CHRISTIAN LIVING
IN THE HOME

CHRISTIAN LIVING IN THE HOME

Jay E. Adams

Presbyterian and Reformed Publishing Company
Phillipsburg, New Jersey 08865

ISBN: 0-87552-016-2

90   25

PREFACE

This book is intended to serve two fundamental purposes. First, I hope that individuals and families will use this book on their own. In the home it may be used to evaluate, discuss, and improve on various aspects of the Christian home. I trust that it will point the way to God's solutions to problems.

Second, this volume has been designed especially as an aid to Christian counselors. It may be used in conjunction with the counseling of husbands and wives, parents and children, or single members of the family. In the counseling of families, chapters may be assigned for reading and discussion between counseling sessions. The assignments at the end of chapters should be completed before the next session. In the case of premarital counseling, counselors may find it useful to assign chapters 4 through 7.

It is my prayer that the Spirit of God will use this exposition and application of His Word to many Christian families for their blessing and for the growth of the church of the Lord Jesus Christ.

Jay E. Adams
Philadelphia, May 1972

CONTENTS

1 A Christ Centered Home 9
2 Hope and Help for Your Family 15
3 Communication Comes First 25
4 Bible Basics About the Family 43
5 Single Persons 59
6 A Word to the Wives 69
7 Loving Leadership 87
8 Discipline with Dignity 103
9 How to Live with an Unbelieving Husband 127
10 Conclusion 139
Scripture Index 142

1

A
CHRIST CENTERED
HOME

Is it possible to have a Christ centered home in today's world of trouble and sin? If you are a Christian you are concerned about this problem. You may be concerned mostly because you recognize that your home falls far short of any such description. If this is true, it is by no means true of you and your home alone. You are in the company of many other Christians who, in their frank moments, will tell you that they too are facing the same difficulty. Let's not fool ourselves. For the most part, Christian homes come pitifully short of the Biblical norms; and we are all aware of it.

Well then, perhaps we should begin by asking the question, What does a truly Christian home look like? Is it an idyllic place where peace and quiet, tranquillity and joy continuously reign? Definitely not! The first and most important fact to remember about a truly Christian home is that *sinners live there.*

The notion that the Christian home is a perfect or near perfect place is decidedly not Biblical. The parents in the home fail; often they fail miserably. They fail one another, they fail their children, and they certainly fail God. The children fail too. They bring home report cards with Ds and Fs, throw tantrums in the shopping mall, and try to eat peas off their knives when the preacher has been invited to dinner. Husbands and wives quarrel, get irritated with one another, and sometimes have serious misunderstandings. Of course, there are accomplishments too; but the point that I want to make is that conditions frequently are far from ideal. That is the realistic picture of a truly Christian home.

Perhaps you are wondering how such a description differs from that of the house next door, in which there is no one who makes a profession of faith in Christ. You may be wondering, "Why did he describe a truly Christian home in those terms?" The answer is simple: this is exactly what the Bible throughout gives us reason to expect among saved but yet imperfect persons. In fact, the whole Book deals from beginning to end with how Christ saves men from their sins. Salvation is complete; it involves justification, sanctification, and glorification. By grace, through faith, God justifies believers in an instantaneous act. That is to say, Christ died for His people in order that the penalty for their sins might be paid and His righteousness might be counted to them. They are declared just before God when they believe. Once justified, Christ saves them from the power of their sins through the *lifelong process* of sanctification. In sanctification, Christians are made more and more like Jesus Christ. But a lifelong process never ends, and the final goal is never reached until death. At death, Christians are glorified; they are then made completely perfect for the first time. But during this life, Christians continue to sin.

"But how," you may insist, "does your description differ from the description of the unsaved family next door?" This question needs to be answered. In the answer lies the message of this book.

A truly Christian home is a place where sinners live; but it is also a place where the members of that home admit the fact and understand the problem, know what to do about it, and as a result grow by grace. Let us look in more detail at three significant differences that make all the difference in the world.

1. **Christians admit their sins.** Because they know the Bible says that no Christian is ever perfect in this life (cf. I John 1:8-10), Christians are able to acknowledge the fact and, in time, learn to anticipate and prepare for sin. They, of all persons, should never rely upon rationalizations, excuses, or blameshifting (although, of course, as sinners they sometimes do) to try to euphemize their sins. They do not have to cover up, for all Christians know that all Christians sin. There can be, therefore, a certain amount of openness, honesty, and relaxation about the relationships that Christians sustain to one another, especially in the home. I am by no means suggesting that we may be relaxed about sin; exactly not that. What I am trying to say, however, is that Christians do not need to spend anxious hours of futile endeavor trying to cover their tracks. They do not need to think up ways to deceive the fellow next door into thinking that they are sterling specimens of humanity. They may freely admit what they know is true: that they have failed to do the will of God. With the freedom to admit the truth comes the possibility of repentance, and with repentance they can expect forgiveness and help from God and from one another. Christians can progress rapidly out of sinful living patterns as a result. They can pour their time and energies into the endeav-

or to replace sinful patterns with Biblical patterns of life. Rather than wasting time minimizing or denying the fact of sin, Christians can concentrate on dealing with sin.

Parents certainly can take a lot of the unnecessary grief out of child raising when, as a matter of course (rather than becoming falsely shocked over the fact), they expect their children to do wrong things at home, at school, and in public. There is then no necessity to subject children to unusual and inappropriate discipline or to the excessive anger that sometimes grows out of embarrassment. Once parents are prepared to admit that the Biblical doctrine of original sin is true not only in theory, but is operative as well in the life of little Mary or Johnny, they can relax and deal with the problem appropriately (Biblically). Again, this does not mean that they will excuse or ignore sinful behavior in their children, or that they will be unconcerned about it as something inevitable and, therefore, about which nothing can be done. No, not that at all. Rather, they will acknowledge sin for what it is and will proceed to deal with it in a Biblical manner. All of which leads to the second difference:

2. **Christians know what to do about their sins**. Because they have the Bible as the standard of faith and practice, Christians not only know why problems occur in the home, but they know what to do about them. Thus the truly Christian home differs from the home next door in that it can use Biblical precepts and examples successfully to handle and recoup from every occurrence of sin. This, again, is a significant difference. The Bible not only contains directions about what to do when one or more members of the family fall into sin; it goes beyond this and shows what to do to assure that there will be no such future failure. Because this book largely is devoted to a consideration of many of the most common problems found in the Christian home, I will not enlarge upon this point here.

3. **Christians progress out of their sins**. Where there is spiritual life, there also will be spiritual growth. No Christian can remain the same yesterday, today, and tomorrow. A fundamental presupposition of the Christian faith is that

there will be growth out of sin into righteousness. Where there is Bible study, prayer, witness, and the fellowship of the saints, the Spirit of God will be at work to produce His fruit. That fruit is righteousness. This book deals also with many of the ways in which the Bible may be used preventively in Christian homes to avoid the trials and problems that the family next door must face simply because they have no such standard.

The Christian home, then, is a place where sinful persons face the problems of a sinful world. Yet, they face them together with God and His resources, which are all centered in Christ (cf. Col. 2:3). Sinners live in the Christian home, but the sinless Savior lives there too. That is what makes the difference!

2
HOPE AND HELP
FOR YOUR FAMILY

There is hope and help for your family. Today we hear much about failure. We are told by pastors, sociologists, psychologists, and a host of others that the home has failed, that parents have failed, that government programs dealing with problems of crime and delinquency have failed, and also that the Christian church has failed. It is not surprising, then, that at times even Christians begin to wonder whether there is any hope for solving the problems of their homes.

Christians, like many others in our society, may find themselves asking, "Can anything significant be done?" They may think, "Have world problems grown so large that at last the situation is hopeless?" Unfortunately, Christians seem to have a tendency to buy what the world sells. If you have lost hope, that may be part of your problem.

Take, as an example, a product that the world has been peddling for some time now, that even many of the most conservative Christians have bought. That product is a viewpoint that blames most of our troubles and failures on sickness. The tragedy is that when the world speaks of sickness, God often talks of sin. For instance, the Bible does not call this world a *sick* world; but that seems to be a favorite designation of people all around us. They keep on saying this in one way or another: "This world is sick; this country is sick; or such-and-such a person is sick." That seems to be the modern diagnosis, and excuse, for most of our problems!

The trouble is, you see, that the medical model (the view that sickness is at the base of most of our problems) has become far more than a metaphor. As a metaphor, or figure of speech, the idea of speaking of sin as a disease is perfectly acceptable.[1] Many Americans understand *sickness* not as a metaphor; they take it literally for a fact. They have been taught to think that a strange sickness is the cause of our basic difficulties. People talk seriously, for instance, about mental illness. But by those words most people mean something entirely distinct from brain damage, which is the only *literal* form of mental illness. They use the words *mental illness* to refer to the problem of youngsters who aren't making it in school, children who are having a hard time with their parents, or a marriage that is breaking up. Such terminology turns a metaphor into a reality. It is a serious error to

---

[1] It is acceptable because it is Biblical. See Isaiah 1:5-6. It is a pity that this Biblical imagery must be used with such caution today for fear of being misunderstood.

speak of sickness or disease when discussing the etiology of a problem when there is no evidence whatever of organic difficulties like brain damage, toxic damage, or glandular malfunction. But heedless of this distinction, modern society has lumped together a great variety of problems under the one category of illness.

To add to the confusion, it is possible for people to become sick (literally) by failing to do what God says about their problems. Worry, for example, may lead to ulcers; fear may cause paralysis; and resentment may trigger colitis. But notice, in such instances sickness is the *result*, not the *cause* of the problem. The cause in each case is sin.

There is something very insidious about calling sin sickness. To call problems that stem from disobedience to the law of God "sickness" or "emotional problems," is to euphemize the Word of God. People may mean well in doing so (they usually do); but as in every instance where one attempts to do evil that good may come, the outcome is destructive. By using what is supposed to be a more gentle or kinder term, one actually plays a cruel trick. Calling sin sickness is not so generous after all; instead, it turns out that what one does by this is to take away hope!

There is no cure for the sickness called mental illness. By calling it a sickness, therefore, you destroy hope, because people know that there is no cure for mental illness. There is no shot in the arm for this strange disease that nobody can isolate. But if you call it what it really is—sin—you will give a Christian hope. If you can genuinely locate the cause of a Christian's problem as a failure to conform to the will of God as it has been revealed in Holy Scripture, you give him living hope. There is little hope if he has been invaded from the outside by a mysterious disease over which he has no control and for which medicine holds no cure. That view of the problem only brings darkness, despair, and gloom. Few persons rejoice when you tell them that they are mentally ill. But if you tell a Christian, "Your problem is that you have been sinning," you give him hope, because he knows that Jesus Christ came to die for sin. He knows that the Christ who died in his place on the cross has the answer to his problem. He knows that there is an answer some place in Scripture. So you do the kindest thing when you call sin *sin*, just as the physician does when he honestly tells the patient that he needs an operation. The sickness model, instead of bringing hope, brings despair.

The medical model also tends to destroy responsibility. A patient says, "I'm sick; I can't help my behavior." Inevitably that attitude plunges him more deeply into sin. He may even attempt to talk himself out of the conviction that he has sinned. He once knew fairly well why he was in trouble; now everyone tells him, "No, you are not responsible," or "You couldn't help it," or "You are sick because of what your parents or society did to you," or "Your problem stems from that traumatic experience somewhere back there in your past," or "You are sick and you should not feel badly about it; you couldn't help it." So he begins to doubt his initial judgment. Finally his conscience may become hardened by such barrages, no longer tender and sensitive to the Word of God. It may become more and more difficult for him to recognize sin for what it is. This may continue until the Spirit of God brings a tragedy or impasse into his life to reawaken the realization that his troubles really have been caused by sin. Why must he experience all of this when he could be spared the agony by calling sin *sin?* What he needs is to repent. He needs nothing less than the significant changes that can be brought about by none but the Holy Spirit. Much heartache and suffering are averted when sin is recognized and labeled as such from the beginning.

In the light of these preliminary observations, let us turn our attention to family problems. *There is hope.* Most family problems are not due to organic illness or anything that legitimately could be called sickness. Organic illness may affect behavior, of course; but such relatively rare difficulties will be exempted from the rest of the remarks in this book. Instead, we will focus on the great number of problems that Christian families are having because of sinful patterns of living. These developed from a failure to study and apply the

Word of God in the power of the Spirit. There is hope, real hope for you and your family. The problems that you have can be solved. There is hope for your family, for your life, and for your children, because God is the foundation of that hope. You do not need to think and talk in terms of failure. Instead you may talk about success, real success, solid success, indeed jubilant success! You have a Savior, and He has given you His Word and Spirit. The Bible has the answer to your problems. By the power of the Holy Spirit you can live according to Scripture. So the first thing to note is that there is hope.

There really is hope. Because of the hopelessness that seems to be abroad among Christian people today, there is need to emphasize this point. Often Christians go to a Christian counselor as a last resort, hoping against hope. Frequently they have visited other counselors, hearing and trying this and that, all to no avail. Again and again they have entertained high hopes, only to have them dashed to the ground. By the time that a Christian counselor sees them, counselees often have taken the posture of stiff-arming hope, holding it at arm's length. They are afraid to hope again, lest hope will come crashing down once more as it has so often in the past. This fact is understandable to every Christian counselor; he works constantly with people who lack hope. You may have this problem. If you too are afraid to hope again, you must come to see that there is hope, in spite of your skepticism, in spite of repeated failures. If you are one of those people who once had hope but found that your hopes were not realized, you need to hope again. But this time you must base your hope on the solid promises and programs of the Word of God. There is hope for solving family problems if you follow God's procedures. Yes, even *your* problem can be solved. That means, for instance, that a problem with your child who has started taking drugs—even that problem—can be solved. There is hope.

You say, "You are very positive; but if you knew my problem, you might change your mind. And besides, why should I trust you? Other people have tried to sell hope to me. Are you sure you are not engaging in some kind of unscriptural oversell?" I can understand and sympathize with your reticence, but I must protest against it because it is Biblically wrong. Let me point you to a crucial passage in the Word of God: "No test has overtaken you but such as is *common* to man, and God is faithful who will not allow you to be tempted beyond that which you are able to bear, but will with the test make a way of escape in order that you may be able to bear it" (I Cor. 10:13). That verse is chock-full of hope. There Paul gives believers all kinds of hope.

Do you understand what God promised the Corinthians? First He said, "I want you to know that I will not call on you to face any problem that is unique." Isn't that wonderful? Jesus Christ, who was "tested in *all* points without sin," has faced your problem successfully. Other Christians who have followed in His steps by the direction of His Word and the power of His Spirit also have faced that problem successfully. That means that by the resources of God you can face it successfully too. One reason why Paul wrote this way was to give hope to these Christians. Shouldn't *you* take hope then?

Now I recognize that some people smile bitterly when you say that there are no unique problems. They think of the differences of culture and geography between Corinth and modern America that time has brought about. They may focus upon the intensity of their own problem. "Nobody has had to live with a husband like mine," they will reply. "Nobody has had to put up with parents like mine," they may retort. "Boy, if you had to handle my kid you wouldn't be talking that way," you may be saying under your breath as you read these words. I think that I know how you feel, but still I say that you are wrong. God is right and you are wrong; He is always right. "Let every man be a liar," but God is still right. And God says there is hope. After you have stripped away all of the superficial top-layer differences—which of course are distinctly personal—there is no problem that is unique. When you boil down problems, the heart of each problem turns out every time to be a common one. At bottom there isn't any unique problem under the sun. There isn't any problem that you or I or anyone else will ever have to face that hasn't always plagued the sons of Adam. There is no problem that has not been faced successfully hundreds of times by other Christians. How can we know? Because God says so. This whole passage stresses the point.

Life in the city of Corinth was as different (superficially) as it could be from the life of the people of Israel back in the Sinai desert. The two could be contrasted starkly in terms of geographic, historical, and cultural differences. Corinth was a bustling metropolitan seaport, in fact a double seaport city, situated on an isthmus. Here is where the world-famous Corinthian games were held. People from all over the Greek-speaking world attended these games. The isthmus connected the mainland to the Peloponnesus, that fingerlike peninsula of southern Greece. The North-South traffic traveled through Corinth, and much of the East-West traffic went through Corinth as well. To travel by boat around the southern shore of Greece was to take an extremely hazardous route. It was safer and easier to discharge passengers and cargo from a ship in a port on the one side of the city, send them both by land across the narrow isthmus, and load them on another boat at the second seaport on the other side of the city.

Corinth was filled with every sort of vice and temptation. Ideas from all over the world flowed into town. As a double seaport, Corinth was a sailor's town par excellence, with all its attendant vice. Corinth was known throughout the world as an immoral city. In fact, one way to insult somebody was to call him a Corinthian.

Well, then, I ask you what could be more different from that kind of community than the affairs of a nomadic people journeying through an isolated desert and living on manna day by day? Indeed, it might be difficult to construct a more vivid contrast than that of nomadic Israel and swinging Corinth. Yet notice what Paul has done. Purposely he set these two obviously contrasting situations over against one another and says that basically they are the same. What happened hundreds of years before to the Israelites is an excellent example, he says, for the Corinthians to follow, because it speaks of common temptations faced by both groups. These things happened to the desert wanderers, but the same things happen in Corinth to you, even though you are living at this late date in history ("upon whom the ends of the ages have come").

You too can safely assume that those things that happened to both the Israelites and the Corinthians are examples for you, although you live in America in the twentieth century. It is not only Israelites or Corinthians who "crave evil things"; modern Americans have the same problem. Those things that happened are "examples" and, therefore, have been "written for our instruction" too. The Bible is relevant; it speaks to us in our time. There is good reason for this. The reason is that nobody at any time in history has ever had to face a truly unique problem. Men of all ages are human beings made by God in His image. God is still the same, sin is still the same, men in every era are still the same. The problems may take different shapes, come in different intensities, appear at different times, or be coupled with other problems in different combinations; but fundamentally they are the same kinds of problems that people always have had to face and always will. That should bring comfort and hope to you. The solutions that God gave to the Israelites and to the Corinthians will solve problems in this modern age also.

We talk about a generation gap today. It is not really a generation gap: it is a generation overlap. That is the problem. It used to be that from one generation to the next there was a long period of time when things happened gradually. It would take several generations for large changes to come about. Changes now take place so rapidly and communication is so fast that the minute an astronaut steps out of his spacecraft onto the moon we all know it; through TV we are virtually there. It no longer takes days in order to find out about significant events; it takes only seconds. People used to talk over a problem for a generation or so; but now before an idea reaches the printer, often it is outmoded. As a result, the generations pile up on each other. The same old problems now come thicker and faster than before. Yet the problems themselves are not unique; they only seem so because we must handle so many more so much more rapidly. That is our particular challenge as Christians today.

Things are changing so quickly that often it is hard to know what to hold on to or what to let go of. But the problems that our fathers faced and that our children will face are no different at bottom. And God, in His providence, has made available new means for handling the added difficulty of bulk and acceleration. This new aspect of the old problems may be met adequately by means of the proper use of rapid transportation and communication, computers, and so forth. In the midst of it all, the basics are still basic. Man's basic problems and God's basic solutions remain unchanged.

Let us then turn our attention to these problems and solutions. We must begin by taking a hard look at the matter of communication in the family as Paul discusses this in the Book of Ephesians.

3

COMMUNICATION
COMES FIRST

In the second half of the Book of Ephesians Paul discusses various relationships between Christians. Beginning at 5:22, he addresses wives and then (25 ff.) their husbands. He describes the fundamental roles and relationships between them. In the next chapter he speaks first to children (v. 1) and then to their parents (v. 4). Finally, he discusses the working or business relationship as he exhorts both slaves (v. 5) and their masters (v. 6). So it is plain that in chapters 5-6 Paul writes about the basic human relationships that Christians, as well as all other men, must sustain.[1]

The first part of the Book of Ephesians (chapters 1-3) concerns the grand and wonderful plan of God's redemption. With a majestic sweep unparalleled in the rest of Scripture, Paul shows how God, from the foundation of the world, planned and in time executed that redemption in the coming of Jesus, who shed His blood on the cross. The wonder of God's love lavished on sinners and the glory of the church of the redeemed in Christ is set forth plainly. But as he begins chapter 4, Paul turns from the more doctrinal and doxological materials to practical exhortations that inevitably grow out of this approach.

Chapter 4 opens with a discussion of the Christian's walk; that is, his daily manner of life as a Christian. On the basis of the great plan of God's redemption in history just unfolded, Paul writes, "I . . . entreat you to **walk** in a manner which is worthy of the calling with which you have been called." In verse 17 the theme is reiterated as he exhorts: "**Walk** no longer as the Gentiles **walk**." In chapter 5 he speaks about **walking** "in love" (v. 1), **walking** "as children of light" (v. 8), and being "careful" how one **walks** (v. 15).

The discussion of the Christian's walk in chapters 4 and 5 must be understood not as a separate subject, but rather as an integral part of the discussion of basic Christian relationships. The walk is not a solitary walk. Rather, it is a walk of one believer with others. When Paul talks about Christian relationships, he is speaking of the joint walk of husbands with their wives, the walk of children with their parents and parents with their children, and of the business man with his

---

[1] Paul followed the same scheme (with variety in emphasis) in the parallel passage, Col. 3:18—4:1. The order in both passages is identical and has to do with the order of life's priorities: husband-wife relationships; then parent-child relationships; and lastly, employer-employee relationships. One's spouse, his children, and his work should be placed in that unvarying order; only tragic results come from reversals or shifts in these priorities.

employees. We do not walk in the paths of righteousness alone. Christ and our brethren are on the road as well. It is the walk of the Christian with the Lord and with other believers that Paul had in mind.

The fourth chapter makes this explicit as the subject of the Christian's walk is introduced. Paul shows deep concern for unity and fellowship in love. He puts it this way: "Be diligent to preserve the *unity* of the Spirit in the bond of peace, *one* body, *one* spirit, *one* hope, *one* Lord, *one* baptism, *one* God and Father of *all*." The stress is on unity—walking together in unity in the name and for the sake of Jesus Christ. The Christian walks as a member of the church, the body of Christ's redeemed people. This redeemed body is not in fact unified, and He has sent His officers to work in her midst in order to bring about the unity of the faith (4:11, 12).

In chapter 4, Paul reminds the reader of his former life (walk). After sketching the discouraging picture, he insists that if one truly has become Christ's, then there must have been a change in his life. In Christ, he has put off the "old man" and put on a "new man." What has happened in Christ must now take place in one's daily walk. Be (in daily life) what you are (in Christ).[2] This is the background, motif, and setting against which Paul will discuss basic Christian relationships. Christian relationships must unify and cause growth not only individually but also corporately, so that the whole body grows into the fullness of Christ and thus, as His body, properly manifests Him to His glory and honor and praise.

But this is a *practical* section (by no means lacking the doxological emphasis) that concentrates upon ways and means. How can a Christian grow in his interpersonal relationships? That is the question to which Paul next addresses himself.

First of all, Paul stresses the need for vital Christian communication as the basic skill needed to establish and maintain sound relationships. A sound husband and wife relationship is

---

[2] Cf. especially the important parallel passage in Col. 3:8-12, where the injunction to be what you are is even more apparent.

impossible apart from good communication. A healthy relationship between parents and children depends on such communication. Businessmen and employees first must learn to communicate in order to get along. That is why the very first subject discussed after exhortations to restore the image of God in one's daily walk is communication.

Paul's analysis of communication begins at verse 25. He urges: "Therefore, laying aside falsehood, speak truth each one of you with his neighbor, for we are members one of another." Christians cannot walk together unless they do so on the basis of honesty, openness, and truth. As members who function together in the same body, we must have truth in order to work in concert. This is Paul's basic point. He elaborates upon this question of Christian communication throughout the rest of chapter 4. We must turn our attention, therefore, to that portion of Ephesians (vv. 25-32).

Communication is fundamental to a Christ centered home because it is the means by which a husband-wife relationship and parent-child relationship is established, grows, and is maintained. Apart from the open channels of truthful communication that Paul discusses here, there can be no truly Christ centered home.

A missionary and his wife returned from the foreign field several years ago. She had become severely depressed. When she came home, she went for a year to a psychiatrist, who talked separately first to her and then to her husband; but nothing ever happened in that experience. Somebody told them about our counseling center, so she and her husband came (we insisted that both of them come together). We began to talk, and as we did she turned to her husband and said: "My problem is that when I married you I didn't love you. I haven't loved you since. I've never loved you, but I've never told anyone the truth before." That missionary and his wife are now back on the field, and they love each other. She loves him and he loves her better too. She had a problem, but nothing could be done to help because she "never told anyone the truth" about it. She did not know how to deal with the problem; and no one else, including her husband, knew what to do. Once communication took place, the problem could be solved. Until then her life had been a miserable, hypocritical farce. The work on the field suffered, she suffered, and her husband suffered. The whole body suffered for want of honest communication. Year after year she suffered; in lonely self-pity she told herself. "If only I had married someone else! I could be out from under his roof, and life would be so different." But pitying herself led gradually to a downward spiral that eventually brought on such a deep depression that her husband found it necessary to curtail his work and at length to return to the United States. The logjam could be freed *only when she finally told the truth.* Once she did, she received help. And the marriage was rebuilt on Biblical love.

Tom and Jill sat across the desk. She said in the most bitter terms, "I am absolutely certain that this husband of mine is cheating on me; he's been stealing from his overtime pay. I know he's been stealing money. And I want to know what he's been doing with it." She had been holding this in for the last four or five months, ever since she had discovered that it had been going on. As a result she had been growing more and more bitter every day. Turning to her husband, the counselor said, "Tom, where did the money go; did you really take it?" Slowly he reached into his pocket, pulled out his wallet, dug down into the secret compartment, and replied, "It's all here," as he pulled it out and threw it on the desk. "I've been saving it for our anniversary for a special treat for Jill."

Something was wrong with communication in that marriage. Jill was ready to break up a marriage over a total misunderstanding. She had failed to communicate her concern over the money until this point, and the concern doubtless arose in the first place out of previous failures of the same sort. The two of them had had such poor communication in the past that they didn't trust each other. Otherwise this problem never could have reached that point.

Phillip came alone to counseling. He had refused to talk to the secretary; he declined when she asked him to answer the preliminary questions on the intake data sheet. He sat for the first half of the session without saying a word. Finally his counselor said to him, "There are people who would like to have this time who really want help. Shall I schedule this hour for someone else? We must not waste it if you don't mean business with God. Now are you ready to tell the story?" In response he finally opened up and said, "I've been through shock treatments, mental institutions; I've been everywhere. I've been depressed, discouraged, and defeated; all kinds of things have been said to be wrong with me. But there is only one thing wrong with me, and I know it. I've had something down in my craw for twenty-two years that I've never spoken verbally before. When I got married it wasn't because I wanted to. My mother insisted on it; that is the only reason I married Margaret. I have secretly regretted every day since." Every time he went into the bathroom and saw the cap off the toothpaste tube or the tube squashed in the middle instead of rolled up from the bottom, he became infuriated. He would fly into a rage or become deeply depressed. Instead of thinking, "There's a toothpaste tube squashed in the middle," or "There's a toothpaste tube with the cap off," he said to himself, "That *woman* has been at it again!" His resentment toward her and his marriage came to the surface in dozens of such small issues. He had never told her or any other human being. The counselor explained how there could be neither happiness nor harmony in a home apart from truth. After spending considerable time explaining how to tell her the truth, mentioning some possible pitfalls and how to avoid them, the counselor sent him home to talk to his wife. "Don't come back until you tell her," he said. She returned with him. They both earnestly dealt with the problem, and after three weeks were dismissed to continue counseling with their pastor. They left acting like newlyweds. Once the truth surfaced and (after the initial shock) they began to do what God wanted them to do about it, the whole situation changed. Their problem was that they had been living a lie. Their marriage was based on falsehood. Only speaking the truth could help.

You may be like Phillip. You too may be holding things inside. You know if you are. You know that there are unresolved matters that break down communication between you and other members of your family. The problem may be between you and your parents, between you and your wife, between you and your husband, or between you and your children. Iron wedges have been driven deeply between you, many of which have rusted with the passing of time. Nothing has been done about them, and you may have suspected that nothing can be. But how can you expect to have a singing marriage when lies cut off communication? You can't. Yet your marriage can sing if you mean business with God. In spite of everything it *can*. You must begin with this passage which says: "Lay aside falsehood, speak the truth each one of you with his neighbor, for we are members of one another."

Where should you begin? Start by admitting the truth to God and to the others involved. Then look at what the next verse has to say: "Be angry but do not sin; do not let the sun set on your anger." This is a quotation from Psalm 4, which is a nighttime psalm. This psalm was intended to remind one that before the close of the day his heart should be flushed clean of all the bitterness and anger of the day. Nothing unforgiven, unsettled, uncovered should be carried over to the next day. Instead, interpersonal problems must be handled on a daily basis so that they do not build up and abscess. Anger itself is not sinful; every emotion is from God and is good when Biblically appropriate. But, "Do not let the sun go down on your anger," Paul says.

Anger may be handled wrongly in either one of two ways: blowing up and clamming up. On the one hand, as Proverbs continually stresses, anger may be turned into sin by blowing up (see 25:28; 29:11, 22, Berkeley). Losing one's temper is sin. It would surprise some to know how many Christian families suffer from the evil effects of such anger. In some psychological circles ventilation is thought to be therapeutic; so in group therapy sessions, in Encounter sessions, in T groups, and so forth, venting of anger and hostility is encouraged.[3] Counselees are being told to get it out of their systems. They are urged, "Do the here and now thing—whatever you feel like doing; just get it out. If there is something inside just yell it out, scream at the next person across the table, systematically unlace him, take his stuffings out and throw them around the room. Hit the pillow if it represents your mother—hit it until the feathers fly!" In all such advice, there seems to be concern only for the feelings of one person; certainly not for the feelings of the one on whom the wrath is poured. The other person doesn't count; at all cost ultimately (to him) the counselee is the one who has to feel better.

Well, there is nothing Christian about such a procedure and attitude. Listen to Romans 15:1, 2: "We should not please ourselves, but each should please his neighbor for his welfare" (cf. Eph. 4:31, 32). Proverbs is very clear about the fact that a man who so vents his wrath is like a city without a wall around it. That is the first extreme to which one can go. Ventilation is plainly un-Christian.

The other (opposite) extreme is the one mentioned in Ephesians 4. Here Paul condemns those who harbor resentments (in the craw for twenty-two years, or two years, or two days). One meets Christians every day who have that problem. No wonder that this problem is raised as a fundamental issue in Ephesians as a basis for discussing husband and wife relationships. Like blowing up, clamming up is sin.

Some counselees not only let the sun set on their wrath, they let many moons go down. Sue and Wilbur came for counseling. She sat there with arms defiantly folded, he nervously shifting from side to side. You could see before either said a word what it was going to be like. She opened the conversation from her side of the desk with these words: "I'm here because my physician sent me. He said that there is nothing physically wrong with me. He said I'm getting an ulcer, but not from any physical cause." All the while her husband sat cowering. Sue reached down into what looked

---

[3] See Jane Howard, *Please Touch* (New York: Dell Publishing Co., 1971).

like a shopping bag (it was her purse), and she pulled out a manuscript that was at least one inch thick, on 8″ x 11″ size paper, single-spaced, typewritten on both sides. She slapped it down on the counselor's desk and said, "There is why I'm getting an ulcer." He said, "Is that a fact?" and took a look at it. He couldn't have read it in a month, even if he cared to. But as he spot-checked through it, flipping along, he saw immediately what it was. It turned out to be a thirteen-year record of wrongs that her husband had done to her. They were all listed and catalogued. Now what would you have said to her?

The counselor looked at Sue and said, "It's been a long while since I have met anyone as resentful as you." She was a little taken back and Wilbur sat up a little straighter. The counselor continued, "This is not only a record of what your husband has done to you [incidentally, subsequent sessions showed that it was a very accurate record], it is also a record of what you have done about it. This is a record of your sin against him, your sin against God, and your sin against your own body. This is a record you cannot deny; you put it down there yourself in black and white. This record of bitterness shows that your attitude has been the opposite of I Corinthians 13, where Scripture says that love never keeps records." Only then was there a basis to deal with problems. Wilbur certainly had to change the wrong things that he was doing to his wife, but on the other hand she had to change the wrong way that she had learned to respond to the wrong things that he was doing.

In most cases of marital disruption, counselors find that it is a matter of sorting out each partner's responsibilities before God. Husbands point at their wives; wives point at their husbands. Usually there is plenty to point to on both sides. But pointing at another hardly solves any problems. To solve problems, husbands and wives should begin by pointing to themselves. Scripture says that one must take the log out of his own eye before he is able to see clearly enough to remove the splinter from another's eye (Matt. 7:3-5). That is exactly where so many go wrong. They attack one another like this:

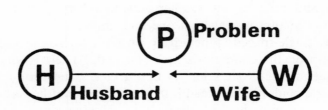

There is no communication when two people are squared off like that against one another. How do you get communication started? Two people communicate when they walk and work unitedly in the same direction:

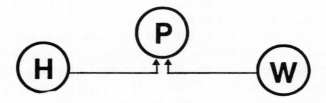

But how do you move the arrows from the former position to the latter? How do you turn the attack from persons toward problems? How may a quarreling husband and wife begin to expend their energy on solving problems God's way instead of continuing along the destructive course of tearing each other and their marriage apart? *That* is the question. The answer is: through the right kind of communication. That is the only answer. They must begin by pointing both of the arrows in the same direction. Either partner may do this by pointing first at himself:

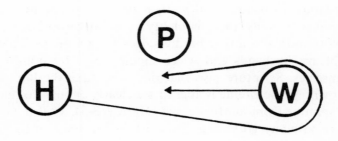

The other arrow is already pointing at you, so all that you have to do is get lined up alongside: look at your own log first. For the first time in a long while the two arrows will be pointing in the same direction. It is truly amazing how much instant agreement you can get from a person who previously may have disagreed with you concerning nearly everything else under the sun, when you begin to say, "*I* have wronged *you.*" Then specify and sincerely ask forgiveness. That is where reconciliation often must begin. You never ought to begin by taking the lid off the other fellow's trash can until you have cleaned out your own garbage can first. That is where communication begins.

Are you having communication problems with another member of your family? Perhaps a flare-up occurred just this week, maybe even today. Could it be with your mother-in-law? Your daughter-in-law? Incidentally, it is not the husband and his mother-in-law who have the most serious interpersonal difficulties, even though that is the relationship that gets top billing in the cartoons. Nearly any counselor will tell you that most problems arise between the two women. This relationship can grow so bitter and can be so terribly disastrous that no one dares to joke about it.

Perhaps your problem is with your parents; maybe it is between you and your child. Is it your husband, your wife, a friend, a member of the church, or a neighbor with whom you have some kind of bad relationship? Listen! You must begin to communicate with that person. If you can't talk to him about anything else, there is always one thing that you can talk about: the wrongs that you have done to him. If you can't think of any wrongs (and I certainly don't want you to cook up any artificial ones), let me suggest one that probably exists. It is simply the one that we have been discussing. If you have been putting off going to another person to try to achieve reconciliation with him, you have wronged him.

Few things are sapping the strength of the church of Jesus Christ more than the unreconciled state of so many believers. So many have matters deeply imbedded in their craws, like iron wedges forced between themselves and other Christians.

They can't walk together because they do not agree. When they should be marching side by side through this world taking men captive for Jesus Christ, they are acting instead like an army that has been routed and scattered and whose troops in their confusion have begun fighting among themselves. Nothing is sapping the church of Christ of her strength so much as these unresolved problems, these loose ends among believing Christians that have never been tied up. There is no excuse for this sad condition, for the Bible does not allow for loose ends. God wants no loose ends. Let us now look at the means He has provided for dealing definitively with such difficulties.

In Matthew 5:23, 24, Jesus says that if you are offering your gift at the altar but you remember that you have done something to another person, drop that gift and go "first" (reconciliation takes precedence over worship) and be reconciled to your brother. Then come back and finish your offering. That is how important it is to get matters settled right away. You must do so right now; do not put it off. Do not "let the sun go down on your wrath" (Eph. 4:26).

Husbands and wives frequently complain that they are having trouble with sex, but the trouble usually is not with sex. Counselors do not find many difficulties that have to do with sex alone. The real difficulties in bed at night come from the fact that all kinds of problems have been carried into bed from the day, problems that should have been settled before going to bed. That is where the difficulties come from; the problems get in the way. Husbands and wives must learn, literally, not to let the sun go down on their anger.

In Matthew 18:15-17, Jesus also says something about the other side of the picture. If someone has wronged *you,* then you must go and see him. You must seek to win your brother and rebuild the relationship so that the two of you can walk together and talk together as Christians. You see, Jesus won't allow the unreconciled condition to continue among believers. In Matthew 5, if another considers you to have wronged him, Jesus says that *you* must go. In Matthew 18, He says that if the other person has done something wrong to you, *you* must go. There is never a time when you can sit and wait for your brother to come to you. Jesus doesn't allow for that. He gives no opportunity for that. It is always your obligation to go. In the ideal situation (the way Jesus set it up), if two believers have flared up over something and they both go away in a huff, when they cool down they both ought to meet each other on the way to seek reconciliation. That is the way it ought to be.

Day by day, week by week, Christians ought to be dealing with interpersonal problems so that they do not pile up. Certainly this is needed preeminently in the Christian home, where there are the most intimate of human relationships, and also where as sinners we run into each other day by day. Like misguided automobiles, we collide and dent each other's fenders, we smash each other's headlights and bang into each other's rear ends. How important it is, therefore, to understand and practice the dynamics of Christian reconciliation in the home. Matters must be straightened out; we dare not ignore them—not even scratched fenders.

Jesus once said, when talking about the future, "Sufficient unto the day is the trouble thereof" (Matt. 6:34). You can't worry about tomorrow. Human shoulders are only broad enough to carry one day's load at a time. If that is true about the future, it is also true about the past. You cannot drag around a lifetime full of unsolved problems and expect to negotiate well in a family. You won't walk straightly. You won't serve very well. You won't do the work of the Lord very effectively if you are carrying such a load. Sufficient unto the day is the trouble thereof. Take up your cross *daily,* said the Lord Jesus; that is, crucify daily the self that is within you. Scripture places a premium on living on a daily basis with God; it makes daily dealing with our brothers an urgent matter.

You don't dare let things go. If there is somebody with whom you are having difficult times or who is having difficult times with you, before this day is over straighten out the matter before God. Write that letter, make that phone call, or if possible pay that visit. In your family sit down and settle matters before nightfall.

Once you get this relationship reestablished, once you have confessed your sins to each other (and to God, of course) and you have asked forgiveness from one another, you have not finished; you have only begun. You have only cleared away the rubble of the past. Now that affairs at last are on a daily basis, you must never allow them to pile up again. That means a new pattern in your relationship must be formed. Paul continues, "Let no unwholesome word proceed [literally, pour out] from your mouth, but only such a word as is good for edification [or building up] according to the need of the moment, that it may give grace to those that hear" (Eph. 4:29). This shows what communication must be like from now on. It is the pattern for forming the new relationship.

What does Paul mean? He is not talking about foul language when he speaks of unwholesome words. Of course his statement would include that, but it is much broader. The term refers to any word that tears down another. Our young people have an expression that closely approximates the idea: they speak about cutting each other up. It is very sad to hear such talk. Christians should never talk about using words—God's great gift for communication—to cut up another. That is what Paul condemns: systematically dicing and cubing another by words.

It is not only youth, but also husbands and wives who use words for such purposes. Sometimes they become quite adept in such misuse of language. Recently a couple attempted to use a counseling session to vent their spleen on each other. Not one word came out of either mouth without a surly, sarcastic remark about the other. Their counselor had to say to them, "That is doubtless one reason why you are here. You may do that sort of thing at home, but I will not allow you to do it here. If you continue, I will close the session." Counselors must not permit such a violation of God's will. Scripture says that the same fountain may not produce both bitter and sweet water. Christians must not take the name of the Lord Jesus Christ upon their lips and at the same time use His gift of words to be nasty to other people.

In the Ephesian passage, Paul describes a better usage for words. Instead of pouring our energies into speech that cuts others down, our words ought to build them up. When words are directed toward the *problem* rather than toward the *person*, they will build him up by helping him solve his problems. Instead of attacking persons with words, a Christian must direct all of his energy, including his words, toward the problem, attacking it God's way.

Look at Paul's thought again: "No unwholesome word" is permissible. Instead, Christian speech involves words that "build up" the other person and that are "according to the problem that has arisen." That means that one's words must be aimed at (or concerned with) the problem that has arisen. Attack problems, not persons, with words.

A husband and wife came for counseling with just such a communication problem. Jan's and Chris's speech was so nasty that unless their attitudes changed, their problems could never be resolved. You see, there are usually at least two problems involved in any human conflict. There is the *issue* over which the parties differ, and there is also the problem of their *attitudes* toward one another. When Chris originally phoned for an appointment he said, "I've got a problem; it is very delicate." He explained the issue that had arisen between him and his wife. This did involve a very difficult matter—one that was quite hard to settle. He said, "I've talked to my minister and he agrees with me. Jan talked to our physician (who is a Christian), and he agrees with her. So we can't get anywhere with either of them. The preacher suggested that I call you; but I know that you are going to take one side or the other, too, so there's no sense coming to see you." "Well," the counselor replied, "I guess there is no sense coming if you have already prejudged me; but if you are willing to come over and let me hear your problems, I want you to know that I don't intend to take anybody's side but God's." Chris mused, "Well, that sounds a little different." So Chris and Jan came. There they sat. During the first few minutes she cut down everything he said and he cut down everything she said. The counselor quickly brought this to a halt. He said, "Look, you have been having problems because of this issue; but the issue itself isn't your major problem. You'll never settle that issue or any other until you first settle the prior problem of your attitudes toward one another. Although both of you profess to be Christians, your present attitudes certainly are un-Christian. Your pastor may have decided the issue for you and your physician may have done the same, but I don't intend to do anything of tne kind. You are going to make this decision yourselves, and in doing so you are going to learn *how* to talk to one another as well. I want you to know also that ordinarily we don't work with anybody longer than twelve weeks. Most leave in eight weeks. I expect you to solve this problem in that time. We will start on your attitudes first." "That sounds different," said Chris in his characteristic manner.

At the time Chris and Jan were not living together. He had left her. "First," the counselor explained, "you will have to go back together again. You can't put two people together by keeping them apart. I Corinthians 7 says that you must be reconciled. To begin with, here are the things you are going to do this week. . . ." They agreed and went to work. They sought and received forgiveness from God and one another. Then they really began to work on the problem of communication. The issue itself was shelved for the time being. When other matters were cleared up and their attitudes were squared away and their marriage really began to take shape again, then they were turned loose on the issue. Chris and Jan went to work on the problem *together*. In previous weeks they had discovered how to use words to solve other problems God's way. They really worked hard on the main issue, and at the eleventh session they announced, "We have solved our problem." And they had! The reason why they couldn't do so before was because they did not know how to communicate as Christians should. They were using words to cut each other up; they were expending their energy by tearing each other apart. When in repentance they began to attack problems with words instead of attacking each other, they discovered the joy of researching issues Biblically. Then the whole picture changed. When communication was straightened out, it was possible for the issue to be solved.

Christians can learn to live without bitterness, wrath, anger, clamor, slander, and malice. They must work on maintaining an attitude of good will toward one another. In the soil of such attitudes solutions to life's problems grow thick and tall. Such attitudes can be sustained only by being "kind to one another, tender-hearted, forgiving one another *just as* God in Christ has forgiven." What a wonderful Savior we have. It wasn't lovely people for whose sake He died; it was for ungodly people, for His enemies. It was for law breakers that He suffered. He loved us, says Paul, in spite of how unlovely we were. *Just as* He loved us, Paul insists, we are to love one another.

Love at first is not feeling. Love first can be expressed as giving. That is at the core of love. If one gives, the feeling of love will follow. To love we must give of ourselves, of our time, of our substance, of whatever it takes to show love; for giving is fundamental to the Biblical idea of love. Listen to this: "God so loved the world that he *gave* his only begotten Son" (John 3:16). "He loved me and *gave* himself for me" (Gal. 2:20). "If your enemy hungers, *give* him something to eat; if your enemy thirsts, *give* him something to drink" (Rom. 12:20). It is always *giving* with which love begins. And that spirit of giving brings a new atmosphere into any home. It is an atmosphere that creates a climate in which communication may grow and thrive. Think about all of this; perhaps there is some action that you need to take. Possibly you need to confess your sin to God and then to somebody else with whom you need to reestablish communication leading to a new relationship in Christ.

BIBLE BASICS
ABOUT
THE FAMILY

The foundations are shaking. There isn't the slightest question that the values and practices of our society are being attacked from all sides. Basic principles as well as the old mores are being challenged. Old ways, both good and bad, are being discarded by young people. Some of the old ways ought to be discarded. Let's be clear about that; many of the old ways were not Biblical to begin with. But we hear also of young people going much further; some are digging down into the roots in an attempt to rip up the very basis of society itself. For example, questions are being asked about trial marriages of two or three years' duration; and some think that marriage, like insurance, should be placed on an annual, renewable basis. When suggestions like that are made in all seriousness, it is time for Christians to reassert the Bible basics about marriage.

The institution of marriage is not a casual one. The study of marriage, of the family, and of home life is the study of the most fundamental and basic institution in society. The church (in its formal sense) was not yet founded when God established the family as an institution. The state as a formal institution was not yet in existence when the family was brought into being. The family is foundational; it was first because it is basic. And it is just because it is first in Scripture that we must make every effort to preserve the family. The guns are pointed at the very existence of the family itself, and we will be in serious trouble if we do not defend it from the attack. It is crucial to such a defense for Christians once again to understand and to reaffirm the basic Biblical principles concerning the family.

The first basic that needs to be reasserted is that *God ordained marriage.* Marriage is not an option. It is quite wrong to imagine that somewhere in a cave around a flickering fire one night a group of previously promiscuous people decided that marriage might be a good idea. It is not a social contract that men worked out and found useful to society for a while. If that were so, we might readily work on better options for the days to come. Indeed, some who hold the optional view think that there are better options. "Marriage was fine for its time," they say; "but now we've outgrown it. We need a bigger suit. Now that we have the pill and legalized abortion, most of the usefulness of marriage has disappeared." No, marriage isn't like that. Many things in life are like that—good ideas just for a time, to be discarded when something better comes along. But marriage is different. Marriage is basic to society because God ordained marriage for all time, not for just a very brief period of the world's history.

The first marriage ceremony was performed in the Garden of Eden with God Himself officiating at the ceremony. It is instructive to notice the word that God uses to describe marriage. That word is *covenant*. In the Book of Proverbs God warns against the adulteress who flatters with her words, who "leaves the companion of her youth and forgets the covenant of her God" (2:17). In leaving the husband whom she married in youth, she is accused by God of forgetting (and breaking) His covenant. Marriage, then, is nothing less than a covenant ordained by God. A covenant in Scripture is a solemn arrangement involving a ruler and a subject. A covenant is imposed on the latter by the former, and entails blessings when kept and a curse when broken. When one enters into a covenant, he enters into the most solemn and binding arrangement of all.

Malachi also refers to marriage as a covenant. God had refused to accept the offerings of His people. They asked why. He replied, "You say for what reason? Because the Lord has been a witness between you and the wife of your youth against whom you have dealt treacherously though she is your companion and your wife by covenant" (2:14). God argues that a wife is a companion and wife *by covenant*. A marriage is a covenant made in the presence of God. God ordained marriage; it is not optional. We cannot do about marriage as we please, whether we please, when and where we please. That is the first, the most crucial, and the most basic factor of all.

Second, because marriage is from God, *marriage is good*. Marriage was instituted before the Fall. The way some people speak about marriage, the way they disparage it and joke about it, one might think that marriage was introduced by Satan. It might be hard for some to believe that marriage is good. By others, marriage is represented as sinful or inferior or a lesser of two evils because of the sexual relationship between married partners. Marriage was ordained by God and sex is good. It was given to bless, to make man happy and joyful. A woman at a Bible conference asked, "Don't you think that the marriage act is nauseating?" The answer is no! Sexual relations are holy, righteous, and undefiled unless perverted by sin. Marriage is good because it is from God. The marriage bed must be kept "undefiled," says the writer of Hebrews (13:4). In Ephesians Paul paralleled the marriage relationship to the holy relationship that exists between Jesus Christ and His church (5:22-33). That is what marriage should and can be like. In the Book of Revelation, Jesus spoke of His relationship to His people as that of a bridegroom to a bride (19:7-9; 21:2). So, then, God considers marriage holy and righteous.

If not unholy, is marriage a lesser or secondary state? Is celibacy preferable? There are those who have so misunderstood Paul's words in I Corinthians 7:26. There he does point out certain advantages of celibacy and disadvantages of marriage. But the reason why Paul discusses the question of celibacy versus marriage is not to make basic generalizations, but to deal with a special situation. Paul foresaw a terrible blood bath about to come on the church. He says, in effect, "All that I'm saying, I want you to understand, refers to marriage in the light of the present world situation." Listen to his exact words: "I think then that this is good *in view of the present distress* that it is good for a man to remain as he is." Paul was not saying that the single state is better than the married state. Paul recommended celibacy over marriage in times of persecution. Persecution was imminent:

> But this I say brethren, the time has been shortened so that from now on both those who have wives should be as they had none; those that weep as though they did not weep; those who rejoice, as though they did not rejoice; those who buy as though they did not possess; those who use the world as though they did not make full use of it (I Cor. 7:29-31a).

Paul was talking about celibacy as an emergency measure. Obviously, it would be easier for individuals than for families to endure persecution. Don't let anybody tell you, therefore, that celibacy is commended in Scripture as a higher state than marriage. Paul wrote in I Corinthians 7 about an exceptional situation; he did not set it as a rule or the norm.

The normal state is marriage, not celibacy. A man and wife—not single persons—were put into the garden. Celibacy is exceptional and it takes a particular gift. Indeed, God specifically declared that "it is not good for man to be alone" (Gen. 2:18). He insists, as the norm, that a man must leave his father and mother and "cleave to his wife" (Gen. 2:24). God ordained marriage for His purposes. Those purposes are outlined in Scripture. It is not possible to enumerate all of them here; there are many and they are varied. But some of those that are most basic must be considered.

In the second chapter of Genesis, these interesting words appear: "Then the Lord said, it is not good for the man to be alone. I will make a helper suitable for him" (v. 18). God then took a rib from Adam and formed woman from it. God made woman as a "helper." Why? Because it is "not good" for man to be alone. If the marriage state were inferior, God never would have uttered those words. The basic, ordinary, and most natural state is the state of marriage. There are those who will live all of their lives outside of marriage. There are people to whom God has given the special gift of celibacy. That is what Paul says in I Corinthians 7. But God created woman for Adam because He said that celibacy was not good. It is, therefore, better for a man to be married. One look at most bachelors' quarters shows (in one dimension) why this is true. However, it is not good for him in any sense. As a rule, man needs a woman.

Now what is a woman? Why, specifically, was she created? Why not just the man? What is it that she must do? She is to be fundamentally (according to v. 18) a *helper*. The King James Version's "help meet" obscures the point. A modern term that developed out of those two words is the elided nonword "helpmeet." We don't understand what a helpmeet is because there isn't any such thing. What the King James Version actually says is "a help [helper who is] meet." Woman was created as a help meet for man. Well, what does that mean? It means a helper who is meet (appropriate for or suitable for man). She corresponds to or complements man at every point. She completes man. A number of different translations of the word "meet" are possible.

God created the woman because man needed her help. That is a Bible basic. She was created as a suitable helper to stand with him in life to help in every way. That is another basic. The idea of woman as helper is a key concept that has been lost in modern marriages. It is a key that has disappeared from contemporary thinking. A woman does not conceive of herself as a helper anymore. Many women think rather of themselves as those who ought to be helped. Or the modern woman thinks of herself as somebody who stands in exactly the same place as her husband. She may have many ideas about her role, but among them she probably does not embrace the notion of herself as a helper. Yet that is God's definitive word about her role.

As we continue, we will see that it is precisely by considering herself a helper that a woman is liberated. Women's Lib movements that fail to recognize this thereby unwittingly consign a woman to a life of slavery. In understanding and living according to her correct role before God and before her husband, she will find freedom. In no other way may a woman truly be liberated. But for now this one thought should be fixed indelibly in your mind: the woman was created to help her husband.

As a helper she complements him, she is suitable for him, she is meet for him, and she completes him. The man and his wife become one flesh (Gen. 2:24). Together they form one complete unit. As they come together physically, intellectually, emotionally, there is a wholeness that did not exist before. They are fused into one. Slice an orange down the middle irregularly. Each side immediately corresponds to the other. When they are joined, they fit exactly. The one exactly corresponds to the other slice, and as both fit together they become a whole. That is the picture in these verses. God created a helper who was exactly fitted to the man He had created, so that when the two would come together they would complete one another and they would be a whole.

Man needed the woman to complete himself. That is why it was not good for him to be alone. Although it is not stated, the woman also needs the man to complete herself. When God gives the gift of celibacy, He provides grace to enable people to live in an incomplete manner. Their completeness must be found in Him. Yet that is not His ordinary way of doing things.

How varied are the viewpoints of a man and a woman on any subject. How much fuller to have both the masculine and the feminine viewpoints available. When each looks at the same question, he (or she) comes at it in different ways. Take the subject of child care, discipline, and training, for instance. The woman comes at it from her perspective. She represents the fiercely loving protection of the mother bear with a cub. She is likely to show her claws when someone threatens her little one. The father, on the other hand, may be more interested in pushing the child out into society to dry him behind the ears. He knows that he has to get a few lumps. It is good for the child to experience both sides of this picture. The balance is important for emphasis and timing.

Incidentally, this subject cannot be discussed at length here; but it is important to insert at least a note. The church of Jesus Christ has failed miserably in helping the single parent. When a woman must raise her children alone without male influence, it is difficult for the child, particularly if he is a boy. It may be that for various reasons she cannot marry again. Thus a covenant child may grow up in the church without a father. The church ought to move in and provide fathering for such children. That child needs to experience something of the fatherly side of a marriage. He needs the men in that congregation. He needs families to invite him over frequently into their family so that he can see a family at work; so that he can see the give and take of a husband and a wife. He needs men of the church to take him places— to go fishing with him, hunting with him, to take him camping. Can you think of a youngster like that who may need *you?*

Now let us ask again, how does a wife help her husband?

She helps by being his partner. She helps by completing him. It is not good for him to be *alone*. But whoever finds a wife, finds a good thing. It is good to have someone to talk to. Companionship, according to Proverbs 2:17 and Malachi 2:14, is a basic purpose of marriage. In both passages, the marriage partner is called a "companion." All of us have a need for intimacy; marriage meets that need. It is good to have someone with whom one may discuss ideas, think through problems, talk about issues, and offer another viewpoint. The wife helps her husband in that way. We all need someone to whom we may intimately open our hearts.

A wife helps also as her husband's biological counterpart. Sex in Scripture is holy, normal, right, proper, and good. In I Corinthians 7:1, 2, Paul stresses the fact that if a person does not have the gift of celibacy from God, he ought to get married. There is nothing wrong with sex; and marriage, indeed, is the proper framework for the expression of it. Sex, according to Scripture, is not unholy of itself, but only when it is misused. It ought never to be used outside of the covenant bond. It should be used freely within this structure. God has so ordained. God strongly encourages sexual relations. Indeed, Paul says in this passage that neither partner has the right over his own body. This forbids both self-pleasure (masturbation) and the selfish withholding of sexual relations from one's partner. Sex was not intended to be self-oriented, but rather partner-oriented. Every self-oriented manifestation is a perversion of sex. Sex may be enjoyed, but only according to the Biblical principle that "it is more blessed to give than to receive." Indeed, the most enjoyable aspect of sexual intercourse is not the personal release experienced in one's own orgasm but rather in the pleasure of satisfying one's marriage partner. Husbands and wives are *required* to satisfy their partners. He may not withhold his body in order to get even with his wife. She may not use sex as a bargaining factor. Sexual relations involve giving one's self freely and fully in love to the other in order to fulfil the other's need. Scripture is not prudish about sex, but some Christians have become prudish. As if they knew more than

God! Scripture is very plain about the sexual obligations of marriage.

There are other aspects of marriage. Another purpose is child bearing. It is wonderful to have the quiver full of children (see Ps. 127). God gives children. They are a "heritage from the Lord." Genesis 1:28 says, "God blessed them and said to them. . . ." How did He bless them? Here are the words with which God blessed them: "Be fruitful and multiply." Those are words of blessing from God. With those words He blessed Adam and Eve. He meant, "I give you my blessing to bear children; fill the earth and subdue it."

There is still more to marriage than this. Some of these basics include very important factors that too often have been overlooked. Because they have been overlooked, there has been untold heartache and sorrow. For instance, the latter part of Genesis 2:24, "They shall become one flesh," too often has been isolated for study. Read also the beginning of the verse: "For this cause, a man shall leave his father and mother and he shall cleave to his wife, and they shall become one flesh." Nothing is more important in marriage than to recognize the crucial nature of the leaving and cleaving process. God says that a man must *leave* his father and mother. He must *cleave* to his wife.

What do those words teach? They are words about breaking up something that is temporary in favor of joining something together permanently. Marriage is the most basic unit in human society. Perhaps nothing that will be said in this book is more important than this. The most basic family relationship is not the parent-child relationship, but rather the husband-wife relationship. God ordained this. In this very verse He says that the man must *leave* his father and mother. That relationship must be severed effectively (not totally, of course, but effectively), so that the original relationship that existed when he was living in the home will not continue. When he marries, a man can no longer sustain the same relationship to his parents that he once did. It must change. He must now become the head of a new decision-making unit that we call the family. He can no longer continue many of the former ties to his parents.

Although he must leave his father and mother, the man must *cleave* to his wife: "What God has joined together let no man put asunder." Unlike the parent-child relationship, the husband-wife relationship is permanent. According to Scripture, it must never be broken. While the parent-child relationship is close, it is never described in terms of "one flesh" or "cleaving" or "perfectly corresponding," or "let no man put asunder." But a husband and wife must join and continue to live in unity of soul, spirit, and body throughout the remainder of their lives. Nothing but death must be allowed to break that unity. It is to be permanent.

Modern society has failed to discover this important distinction. In our society, the parent-child relationship has become the more significant one, to the detriment of children and marriage partners alike. Yet, God put a husband and his wife in the garden, not a parent and child. Contemporary parents all too often live for their children. They are urged to give their best time and energies and money and thoughts to their children. The tragedy of it all is that in doing so they seriously deprive their children. Many evils follow the attempt to make the parent-child relationship basic. Family life cannot escape the consequent suffering, since the attempt is in direct opposition to God's Word. The relationship reversal hurts in a hundred ways.

Parents who have built their lives around their children frequently end up in our counseling center around the time when the last child is leaving home. Because they have lived for their children all these years, their talk, their interests, their schedules, indeed, their whole life structure has been built around the children. Then when the children leave home, they suddenly awaken to the fact that all that they have left is each other! They are going to have to spend the rest of their days together, and they dread it. What is left is two strangers who have little or nothing between them except the children. They have failed to build a marriage throughout all of these years. Their marriage was held together by the children. They have built only in one direction. That which was significant in their marriage was matters concerning the children. That was where talk and activities centered.

The most harmful thing parents can do to their children is to build their lives around them. A wall plaque reads: "The best way to be a good father to your children is to be a good husband to their mother." That is exactly right. What children need to see is not indulgent parents who squander all of their love and concern on them. It is wrong (even for the children's sake) for parents to spend the lion's share of their time and interests (even mainly) upon their children. Children need most to see parents who know how to love and live with each other. That is the most precious gift that parents can give to their children. How else will children learn how to build solid marriages for themselves? They need to see parents who know how to live *as parents;* but even more—*as husbands and wives.* Every child needs parents who are concerned about each other.

What happens to children who leave a home in which the parents have lived principally for them? If mother has lived for her son Johnny, she will find it difficult to let him go. Beyond the normal difficulties that grow out of parting, she will have far more. She won't be willing to let go, and so she is likely to hold on to one arm as his wife takes hold of the other. Johnny may allow them to pull him to pieces in the struggle, with tragic consequences for all who are involved. The two women may begin to fight. Or, they may develop deep resentments toward each other or Johnny. Why is it that jokes and cartoons concern the husband and his mother-in-law? One reason may be because that is the only relationship that humorists dare to talk about. The real problem, counselors find, is rarely between the man and his mother-in-law; it is usually between the two women. That is where feelings grow bitter. Frequently this is because of the violation of God's rules about leaving and cleaving.

When a young man allows himself to be pulled apart by his mother and wife instead of obeying the Word of God, everyone suffers. If he leaves and cleaves, in spite of what she says, it is always best for his mother, as well as for his wife and for himself. How crucial it is for mothers to know when it is time to tell the children to leave the nest. They must first teach them how to fly, then nudge them out when the time has come. It is important, then, for parents to understand that the most basic relationship is between the husband and the wife, not between the parent and his child.

Perhaps a word to young people would be appropriate. If you want to do the best for yourself and for your parents, you will not demand so much attention and interest from your parents. You will not be anxious to squeeze every second that you can out of them. They have only so much time. They need to spend some of it with each other. It would be great for some of you now and then to say, "Mom and Dad, I want you to go out and do things on your own. I'll be glad to babysit voluntarily." You should do everything that you can to help your parents to find some time for each other. They need to do some things alone. Not only will your parents benefit, but in the long run this will greatly benefit *you.*

When the time comes for you to leave home they should be looking forward to your leaving. That's right; that is the way it should be. They will know that you are capable enough to start a new life for yourself and they will have a life of their own that they are anxious to enlarge. Parents ought to be saying to each other now and then, "My, won't it be great when the last one is gone. Then we can spend more time together; we will really be together again at last." That is the way parents ought to think. And they will think that way when they consider their marriage to be the most basic permanent relationship of life. Other relationships can be only temporary. God lends children to parents for a while to prepare them for the future; then off they must go. They should be a joy, but they cannot be the foundation of joy in a marriage.

This point truly is crucial. How can it be stated strongly enough? Husbands and wives, ask yourselves this question, what kind of life would you have right now were your children suddenly taken from you? Seriously, what kind of life would you have as husband and wife together? What have you really built between you? Do you have common interests? Do you do things together? What common causes are you furthering? What would you talk about when you sit down at night? What is there *now* between the two of you? That is the question. If you find it difficult to think about what you would say or do, you'd better start working on the problem right now! More quickly than you realize, your children will leave the home. Suddenly college—then comes that girl—and wham! He's gone. Along comes that fellow, and at the snap of a finger she has gone. It will happen just like that, before you know it. And when it happens, you are going to be alone with each other. You can dread the day or look forward to it and plan for it.

Before reading farther, stop and think about this matter. Perhaps you will discover that you need to talk to your husband about it. Possibly you need to speak with your wife. You young people might want to go home and lovingly say to your parents, "Mom, dad, you know that I am going to be leaving you pretty soon; my hope chest is all packed. What can I do right now to help you make your marriage go better? What can *I* do?" How many ways during a given week can you step in and let the two of them find some time alone? Could you cook the meal for *them?* Later on one night after you have eaten, could you serve mom and dad alone by candlelight? Think creatively. Now wait a minute. Did you register sheer disbelief? Don't you think that there is still some romance left in mom and dad? If there isn't, maybe that is because they have been squeezed dry or worn thin in laboring over you kids. Why not do something about that? Make a few offers. Surprise them. Let them know that you care.

And, mom and dad, think about this matter. Dad, when did you last do something with your wife alone? When was it? And the time before that? How long was the space between these two dates? Is there anything that you do regularly? One husband and wife that wanted to get away together found that they had to resort to such unusual expedients as going out for breakfast on Saturday mornings. Whatever it takes, parents must find the time for one another. The obligation to see that this happens falls most strongly upon the husband as the head of the home, for in the final analysis Christ has made it *your* job (as we will see later) to see that the right things happen in your home. It is of vital importance, then, for you to see to it that the relationships in your home are Biblical. If as you consider this matter you find that something is wrong, why not take your wife out to supper tonight and discuss the question?

FAMILY TIME AND INTEREST DISTRIBUTION

In the spaces below make a rough estimate of the amounts of time and numbers of interests devoted to your spouse and to your children. Quantitative factors are only one rule by which to determine whether your time and interests are properly distributed. It is important to judge the quality of the time and the interest items that you enter.

TIME devoted to:		INTERESTS in common with:	
Husband/wife	Children	Husband/wife	Children
Weekdays:			
Weekends:			

On a separate sheet, rework your schedule in a more Biblical manner wherever necessary. When you are finished, speak to your husband or wife about this matter, showing him (her) your proposals.

SINGLE PERSONS

Finding a Mate

It is plain that God in His Word has set forth marriage as the normal state for adults. God did not intend for Adam to remain a single person when He placed him in the garden. After creating Adam, God commented, "It is not good for man to be alone." It is not wrong, therefore, for a single person to desire or seek to be married; that is as God has ordained. Each individual has his own gift from God, whether it be to lead the married life or the single life. If one who has been given the latter gift seeks to be married or is discontent with his lot, he sins, just as when one who has been given the gift of marriage fails to exercise this gift. Each one must discover his own gift from God and live accordingly. God's gifts are not given capriciously; neither are they given in such a way that the option for their use is left with us. As the gifts are discovered they are to be developed and used to the full in His service and to His glory. God distributes His gifts for His purposes and for the good of His people. His sovereign administration of these gifts must be acknowledged as right and proper by His people, even when they cannot see the good. "All things [even gifts for marriage or for the single life] work together for good to those who love God, who are the called according to his purpose" (Rom. 8:28).

Frequently single Christians rebel against their state. They want to be married and deplore their celibate condition. What can be done about this all-too-frequent situation? Several things. First, let the church acknowledge that far too little has been done to provide wide, significant contacts for young unmarried Christians. In her repentance the church should "do works fitting for repentance" by beginning to do a great deal more for singles. The possibility needs to be explored of holding retreats, rallies, intercongregational meetings—even perhaps providing for Christian dating services—and a host of other creative ways for enabling young unmarried persons to find suitable mates. Parents, too, must assume an obligation to help. Perhaps arrangements of various sorts in which children can meet can be worked out by families. (Note the father's prominent part in I Cor. 7:36 ff.) It is high time that much more is done.

But what of the single person himself, or (as is most frequently the case) *her*self? Specifically, what can a young unmarried Christian woman do? This is a practical problem that needs to be addressed directly.

First, she must discover her gifts. Following closely the data mentioned in I Corinthians 7, which recommends celibacy in times of persecution (see vv. 26, 29), she may examine her gifts, focusing for instance on her *desire* (see vv. 2, 8, 9). In most situations, since marriage is the normal state, in conditions of nonemergency, the girl will have the gift of marriage. In that case, she should develop this gift and use it. More will be said presently about this. If she has been given the gift of living as a single person, she must be willing to do so, prepare to do so, and look for the work in the Lord's vineyard that doubtless He has for her. She must not dread the future, looking at it apprehensively, but must recognize that the Lord never calls His children without providing them the help that they need to accomplish His will and the ability to be happy in doing it.

But what of the girl, now twenty-six or twenty-seven, who yearns for marriage and yet has not found that Christian man? What should she do? If she has first determined that so far as she can discover she has the gift of marriage, she must then do at least three things.

1. *Pray about the matter.* You protest: "I *have* prayed! What do you think I pray about all the time?" I know you have prayed—but did it *stop* there? So often young Christian women have developed an unscriptural attitude toward prayer. They think that they must depend upon prayer and prayer alone; any further action on their part would be "unspiritual." When you pray for your daily bread, do you then sit back under a tree (arms folded) and wait for it to drop from the sky on a parachute? "No, of course not," you reply. O.K., then. If you pray and then go to work, you receive your daily bread *as an answer* to your prayer. God ordinarily gives such answers *through* (and not apart from) *your work*. Your prayer, in effect, means, "Lord, give me the opportunity to work, the health to work, and bless my work." Prayer, then, must be coupled with effort: "If any man will not work, neither should he eat" (II Thess. 3:10). That is true even if he prays, "Give me this day my daily bread." The same holds true for a single woman seeking a husband. She should pray, but she also must work at finding him. All of which leads to two more factors.

2. *Prepare yourself for marriage.* If you are reasonably sure that God has given you gifts for marriage, then begin to develop these gifts. This means at least three things. First, develop your abilities to do domestic duties to the full. Learn to cook and sew, spend time with children, and so forth. Second, learn how to become as physically attractive as you can. If you need to go on a diet, then do so; if you do not know how to choose clothes that are best for you, or to fix your hair as you should, learn how to do so. But do not become hung up on the matter of physical attraction. While you ought to be as attractive as possible (a bride is to be "adorned for her husband" [cf. Rev. 21:2; cf. Rev. 19:7, 8, where the bride is described as "making herself ready" for the bridegroom]), you must not put great stock in physical beauty. Read especially Proverbs 31:30 and I Peter 3:3-5. This leads to the third and most important point of all: develop your Christian personality. You must become a vibrant Christian woman. A vital Christian, radiating that hidden beauty of the heart, is more attractive to the right sort of Christian man (the only kind you want) than the raving beauty who is hollow within. A woman who is developing her domestic abilities, who is reasonably attractive, and who is a vital Christian in her own right is an irresistible person!

3. *Proceed toward your goal.* "What?" you say; "should I *do* something toward finding a man?" Let me ask in reply: "Should you *do* something toward earning your daily bread?" A secretary not only prays for work and prepares herself to become an efficient secretary, but she also *seeks* a job! You must *seek* a husband.

How? That is the big question. First, let me warn you. Don't join the single women's gripe group where others go to bemoan their fate but do nothing about it. Such talk engenders bitterness, despair, and depression. You have no time for any such thing; you have work to do. If you already belong, quit promptly!

Go where Christian men are. Choose a job that will bring you into contact with Christian men, even if it pays less money than the one you currently have. Attend retreats and

Bible conferences that will give opportunities to meet Christian men. Of course, this should not be your only (or perhaps even major) purpose in attending; yet there is no reason why it cannot be one purpose and one reason in particular for choosing this type of Christian fellowship and experience in learning. Perhaps you should enroll in a Christian college. "What? Go to college to find a husband? Isn't that an unworthy motive?" This motive should be high on the list of reasons for a woman to attend a Christian college. Ask your pastor to help you discover where Christian men are. He may even know of Christian men who are looking for eligible Christian women. The word should be out among Christian families in your church. They may be able to invite you into their homes along with eligible young men. Speak to married women whose Christian witness you respect, especially those who married later in life; and ask them how they solved the problem. You may get some very helpful advice.

Whatever you do, *do* something about your situation. Be sure that what you do honors God and conforms to His Word. There is every reason to expect that if God truly has given you the gift of marriage, and if you have developed your domestic skills, and if you have done all that you can do to make yourself attractive, vital, and available—all in the spirit of prayer—there is every reason to expect God to send you the right man at the right time. It is then that you may settle back in confident quietness and wait for God to work. He may still want to prepare you in ways that you do not understand. There may yet be disappointments after expectations; but if you know that you have done all that you can do and that you have prayerfully committed the rest into God's wise hands, you can be assured that the outcome will honor Him and bless you.

To sum up then: discover your gifts, develop your gifts, and demonstrate your gifts.

The Myth of Compatibility

Compatibility is a dangerous word. It does not occur in

Scripture, and the concept—as normally set forth in contemporary writing and as used in popular parlance—is quite misleading and unscriptural. The common concept of compatibility, when followed by Christians and non-Christians alike, can lead to disastrous consequences.

What is meant by compatibility? Ordinarily when one uses the word in modern speech he means that two persons have personalities, interests, or backgrounds that are compatible and that, therefore, they would be more likely to make a good marriage than if these elements in each were diverse. There is no evidence in Scripture that this is true. To think that because socio-economic levels are similar or because both persons like tennis or because both fathers wear gray flannel suits to work, these factors will give a young couple the edge in marriage is an idea without Biblical foundation. The entire concept of compatibility must be reexamined Biblically.

The Biblical fact is that no two persons are compatible, regardless of whether their backgrounds were similar or not. We are all born sinners, and that means that we are by nature incompatible people. For two people to be compatible in any true sense of the term means that they first must become Christians and then work (by God's grace) hard at the task of *becoming* compatible. People are not born compatible, they only become compatible by the sanctifying work of the Holy Spirit in their lives.

How, then, may one know how to choose a mate? There are only two absolutely essential requirements: first, that the other person is also a Christian; second, that the two of you not only desire to but growingly give evidence of an ability to face, talk over, and solve problems together from God's Word in God's way. While socio-economic, ethnic, chronological, and other factors may rightly enter the picture as minor matters of preference, they are in no sense essentials. Indeed, they are icing on the cake. The one factor—beyond salvation—that is truly essential is the ability to solve problems Biblically. With this capability, persons with quite diverse backgrounds find it possible to enrich their own lives profoundly.

Difference (or similarity) is a matter of preference, not an essential. But apart from the desire and ability to solve difficulties Scripturally, carbon copy backgrounds will not make two sinful persons compatible.

Therefore, before making any commitments, test yourselves by the acid test: can we together work out the problems that we have been facing as Christians should? Nothing is more essential than this. All through the years you will continue to face such difficulties. The vital question then will not be whether both fathers drove VWs or Chryslers, but it will be: "Can we solve problems together God's way?" Steer clear of any potential marriage partner who wants to avoid solving problems, who wants to minimize difficulties, who wants to follow the Joneses' solutions, or who cannot work together with you using Biblical principles to reach God-honoring answers. Apart from some clear indication that this Biblical problem-solving factor is present and shows promise of further growth and development, go slowly. If there is no evidence of its presence and no change, halt proceedings toward marriage; then tell the other person why you have stalled progress. If there is still no desire to change at this point by dealing with *this* problem Biblically, start looking elsewhere.

When the desire to solve problems Biblically seems to be present but the ability to do so is lacking, one of the two following explanations may describe what is happening: (1) The other party either does not really desire to learn how to solve problems God's way, or if the desire is there, does not have enough motivation to pursue matters until there is a change. Again, if this is the situation, do not become involved unless an actual change occurs and subsequent growth in problem solving is evident. (2) The other party may not know what to do to change. Here good counseling, mutual effort, and so forth will finally prevail. In this case be patient, work hard at the problems, and get whatever genuine help is available. Nevertheless, do not enter into any commitments until the change has occurred and some elements of growth are apparent. Remember, whenever God is at work, He gives not only the desire but also the ability to carry it through (see Phil. 2:13; II Cor. 8:10).

Of course, all of this may also apply to you yourself. Until you too have the desire and the basic know-how and are working at Biblical problem solving in all of your relationships in life, *you* are not yet ready for marriage.

THE SINGLE PERSON'S PERSONAL INVENTORY

In the spaces below make an honest evaluation of your personal qualifications for marriage and list suggestions concerning what you must do as a Christian to become prepared for marriage.

AS I NOW AM

WHAT GOD WANTS ME TO BE

HOW I MAY BECOME WHAT I SHOULD BE

Consider particularly these areas:

PRAYER

PREPARATION FOR MARRIAGE

    Domestic
    Physical
    Christian Personality

PROGRESS TOWARD THE GOAL

CRITERIA FOR MARRIAGE

Is_____saved? ☐ Yes ☐ No ☐ Not Sure

Marriage should not take place unless you can check Yes with confidence.

Do_____and I truly desire to solve problems God's way? ☐ Yes ☐ No ☐ Not Sure

Have we demonstrated that we know how to do so together? ☐ Yes ☐ No ☐ Not Sure

Again, marriage is not indicated until you can check Yes with confidence.

WORKSHEET

List below the solutions to at least five problems that you solved together God's way. These should be problems where you had differences of opinion, difficult decisions to make, arguments, or personal antagonisms to overcome.

PROBLEM	SOLUTION	HOW REACHED

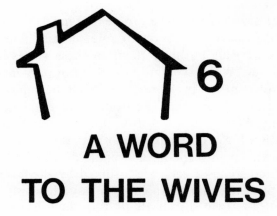

6

A WORD
TO THE WIVES

It was necessary to discuss the fourth chapter of Ephesians, not only to study communication, but also because the fifth chapter must be approached through the fourth. The importance of communication to husbands and wives who seek to function together as Christ and His church should function must not be minimized. Apart from communication they could not work out their proper roles and relationships in the home.

Nowhere else in Scripture are the proper roles of husbands and wives described in such detail as in Ephesians 5. These are the crucial verses that, based on the creation ordinances, expand the Christian's concept of marriage. There are two sections to this passage: verses 22-24 and verses 25-33. We will consider the first section in this chapter. It is God's Word to the wives, which should be sufficient:

> Wives, be subject to your own husbands as to the Lord, for the husband is the head of the wife as Christ is the head of the church, he, himself being the Savior of the body. But as the church is subject to Christ, so also the wives ought to be to their husbands in everything. —Eph. 5:22-24

Almost without exception we have found in counseling that when there have been other serious problems in a marriage, there also has been the problem of husband-wife role failure, usually taking the form of role reversal. The husband-wife roles as Paul outlined them in these verses have not been followed. When they are not, this not only makes it difficult to solve other problems, but itself becomes the source of additional problems. The destructive dynamic is self-propagating. When other unsolved problems come into a marriage relationship, husband-wife roles somehow seem to get thrown up into the air and come down like tossed salad. In the end some of each are assumed by the husband and some by the wife, in a temporary, uneasy, dissatisfying, and unsatisfactory truce. Reversals of role then lead to further problems which often lead to further reversals, ad infinitum. It is important then to understand the proper role of each marriage partner and how to develop and maintain it in a Christian home.

The heart of these words to the husbands and to the wives can be reached quickly by asking two questions: Husbands, do you love your wives enough to die for them? Wives, do you love your husbands enough to live for them?

That is what the latter part of Ephesians 5 is all about. The husband must learn to love his wife as Jesus Christ loves His church. A husband, if need be, should be willing to give up his life for his wife. On the other hand, a wife should so love her husband that she is willing to *live* for him. She must be willing to pour her life into being his helper. This involves living for him, just as the church is required to live for Jesus Christ. Now those are both very large requirements. They are not easy; yet they are the requirements that God set down in this passage. He who laid down the requirements for each role also knows how to help us meet those requirements.

Wives, God expects you to love your husbands so much that you will willingly subject yourselves to them in the same way that the church is to be subject to the Lord. You may object: "Now wait a minute. Don't tell me you are really going to go that route! Do you mean to say that at this late date in the world's history you are going to truck out all of those old words of Paul? Are you going to try to tell us that women are to live that way today? Do you mean to say that in this day of Women's Lib you would dare to talk this way to women? Don't you know that this passage came out of an ancient, backward culture? We don't live in the Orient, where women walk three paces behind their husbands. Get with it! We live in modern America! You can't really mean what you seem to be saying, can you?" Yes, I do. You may further reply: "Well, then, not only was such teaching restricted in time and space to a particular culture, but remember it stemmed from Paul, that old bachelor. It was Paul's fault that this kind of thinking ever became current. After all, Paul hardly knew what he was talking about. He was either married at one time when he became a member of the Sanhedrin, but his wife died and he forgot what marriage is like, or he always was a bachelor and somehow was admitted as an exception. At any rate, when he wrote he didn't know what marriage is all about. He was writing as a single man." But such talk is highly dangerous. Ephesians 5 is the inspired Word of God. Paul was writing under the moving power of the Spirit. Ladies, if your fur bristles and the claws begin to show, don't blame me; don't blame Paul. This is God's Word.

As a matter of fact, many calumnies have been brought against Paul. These are a disgrace not to Paul, but to the Christian women who speak so unthinkingly. No writer in the New Testament says more gracious things about women than the apostle Paul. I urge you to look at his letters some time. Look at the closing chapters of the Book of Rómans, for instance. Notice in other letters, when he speaks appreciatively about people, how frequently he commends women. He must have had many women as close friends; obviously women in his day thought highly of him. To call Paul a woman hater or an old bachelor who didn't know what marriage is all about is to misunderstand totally Paul's words and thought.

Paul loved women. He was not motivated by a belligerent spirit to write these words or those that he penned to the Corinthians or to Timothy (I Cor. 14; I Tim. 2). He had a larger reason for saying what he said. We can't pass these words off, then, as the thinking of a wizened old bachelor. Nor can they be bypassed as culturally determined. Paul's views regarding women were consistent. When he argued for the subordinate role of women in I Corinthians and I Timothy, he did not base the argument on the mores of his culture. Rather, he went back to creation and the Fall. He said, "The man was created *first*, then the woman." He pointed out that the man was not created for the woman, but the woman was created for the man. He appealed to the order of creation. Paul obviously depended on the Genesis account, where the order of creation is set forth very plainly. Paul did not need to appeal to the Mediterranean culture of the Orient or Greece or Rome. He appealed to creation itself, to the way that God sorted out roles in the beginning.

Then he added a second reason. In I Timothy 2 he observed that not only was woman subject to man by the order and purpose of her creation, but he noted also that it was not the man but the woman who first sinned. He appealed to the order in the Fall and to the declaration of God to Eve following the Fall: "Your husband will rule over you." On those two fundamental accounts Paul based his discussion of the husband-wife roles. Man was created first, and woman was created to be his helper. Because of what Eve did, God also declared that men must rule over their wives. So, then, it was not on cultural considerations, but on the most basic factors of all—creation and the Fall—that Paul based his discussion in Ephesians 5. Nothing less, nothing different, nothing more than this is behind his words concerning submission. Having cleared away such objections, it may now be possible to consider the passage carefully, together with its present-day implications. But don't hastily jump to conclusions. You may be pleasantly surprised at what Biblical submission really means.

Paul begins with these words: "Wives, be subject to your own husbands as to the Lord." That is a strong statement. The same way that you would be subject to your Lord is the way that you should seek to be subject to your husband. He continues, "For the husband is the head of the wife, just as Christ also is the head of the church." Christ rules His church; He is the head over it. He gives it direction and speaks a word of authority to it. Finally he explains, "As the church is subject to Christ, so also the wives ought to be to their own husbands in everything." People have tried to read this some other way. They have tried to dull the edge. They have twisted it and ignored it. But there is no way to get away from the plain intent of these words, no matter how you squeeze them. Again and again in those three sentences Paul tells women that they must submit to the authority and rule of their husbands in the home. They are to be submissive. Elsewhere in Scripture the same message is repeated by Peter, who was a married man (I Peter 3:1ff.). No one can accuse Peter of being a woman hater.

You must understand what submission means, since you must obey the commandment whether you like it or not. That means *you*, Christian woman: you must obey your husband; Christ says that you must. There is no option about it. He doesn't say that it would be nice for you to do this. He doesn't say that everybody would be happier if you did so. He doesn't say that homes would run more smoothly if you obeyed. He says that you *must* obey. You must obey, not primarily for the benefits that you and your husband will receive, but *in order to exhibit the relationship of Jesus Christ to His church.* At all costs you must not misrepresent this relationship. You cannot exemplify the love that the church must have for Jesus Christ if that kind of love is not in your heart for your husband. And it must be seen in your submissive life as a result.

You may look on this as a tall order. It is. All of your worst fears that Paul might really be telling you that you have to obey your husband may have been confirmed. Over and over Paul repeats the need for submission. Why does he keep on saying it? Because many people keep on not hearing it. That may be why Paul said it three times in three verses in three different ways. He underscored it so that his readers could not miss the point. There is no way to squirm out from under it or to bypass it or hedge over it. You can't do that. You are going to have to live with it, live by it, and live in it. So, let's try to understand it.

To begin with, there are some misapprehensions that must be cleared up. Submission does not remove freedom, it allows for it. When is the train freer—when it is bumping over the hillside *off* the track, or when it is smoothly running *along* the track, confined or restricted, if you will, to the track? It is freer when it is where it ought to be, doing what it was intended to do. *Restricted* to the track means freedom. *Confined* to the track means ability to perform as it was intended to perform. What really brings freedom? Getting on the right track. When is a person freer in playing an organ or piano? Is he freer to learn to play a musical instrument when he says, "Forget the rules and the laws of harmony, the chromatic scale, and so forth"? He is not free when he says, "Forget it all," but rather when he spends the long, difficult hours practicing his scales. "How can this be?" you ask. The one who sits down to an organ and says, "Forget the book and forget the practice" is not free. He pulls out the stops, puts down one foot with a terrible growl. Then his hands come down like thunder—with a squeal and bellow and grunt.

The result? Sheer cacophony! Noise! He cannot play the organ. He is not free to make music. That man isn't free; he is bound by his own ignorance, bound by his own lack of skill, bound by the fact that he has not spent the hours that are necessary to learn how to make music. But the man who takes the long, hard road of restriction, who works *within* the structure, finally arrives at the point where he may throw away the books and write his own music. Freedom in God's world never comes apart from structure. When one is free to live as God intended, he is truly free indeed. We hear much about women's liberation today. I want you to be liberated. Here is the path of genuine liberation for a woman: submission. Submission allows her to run *on the track;* it allows her to make beautiful music in her home.

When you do what God intended a woman to do, when you are what God intended a woman to be, that is when you will be most free. In God's round world you cannot live like a square without having your corners knocked off. It just isn't going to work. You can try to live out of shape. You can try bouncing over the field, off the track. You can try sitting down to the organ with license (which you may wrongly call liberty), but you will not be free.

The principle of submission runs through all of life. It pertains to relationships within the church, as well as within the home (see I Tim. 2:11-15; I Cor. 14:34, 35). A woman is never to take a position of authority over men as a teacher or a ruler. Thus the two works of the elder are denied her. This is not asserted on cultural grounds, but on the basis of the order of creation and the circumstances involved in the Fall.

But what does submission involve? That is the major problem that needs to be solved. Distorted views are rife and must be straightened out. Christians themselves have wrongly interpreted Scripture on this point. They have placed on women burdens that the Bible never intended. They have crushed gifts and stultified ministry that could have brought great joy to homes and rich blessing to the church. A true picture of what the Bible is talking about when it speaks of submission, therefore, is essential.

One idea of submission that is widespread is that submission reduces the woman to the level of a piece of property. She is chattel owned and operated by her husband. She must bow and scrape before him, never offering a suggestion or objection of her own. She must not open her mouth or her mind. She must do his bidding without question or suggestion.

That is not a Biblical picture. That may be an Islamic picture; that may be an old Japanese picture; but it is not a picture that comes from the Bible. That picture utterly fails to represent the Biblical notion of subjection. Biblically the woman is not to be squashed under the heel of her husband. 'Her God given gifts must be neither ignored nor suppressed. Indeed, exactly the opposite picture appears in the Bible.

In order to understand this, let us turn first of all to a crucial passage that explains the husband's role as head, I Timothy 3:4, 5. In this portion of the letter Paul is discussing the qualifications for elders. Elders must be chosen from among men in the church who, in their own lives, exemplify what God requires of all. What does such a man look like? For one thing, Paul says, he must be a good husband and father. If he cannot exert Christian leadership as a head of his home, he will not be able to rule well in the church. What does good leadership in the home look like? Paul says that it consists of managing one's own household well, keeping his children under control with all dignity.

The key word in this description of successful headship is the word *manage*. The husband's job is to manage his family. That is the best translation of the word *proistemi*. The idea is "to preside over." The picture is of one who has control but does not do everything by himself. As the elder is to be a manager of a congregation, so the husband is to be a manager of his home. A good manager knows how to get other people to do things. He knows how to spot, develop, and use the gifts of others. That is what a manager is and that is what a husband is to be.

The husband as the head of the home is its manager. He is the head; the head does not do the work of the body. The husband is not to answer every question or think every thought for his wife—exactly not that. Rather, he is to recognize that God gave him a wife to be a helper. A good manager will look at his helper and say, "She has certain abilities. If I am going to manage my household well, I must see that every last one of those gifts is developed and put to use as fully as possible." He will not want to squash her personality; rather, he will seek to bring it to the fullest flower.

If he is not a mathematical whiz, he will thank God for sending a wife with mathematical ability; and he will make full use of it. He would be a complete failure and a mismanager if he did not put his wife's gifts to work in keeping the books and paying the bills. This is not an abdication of his position; he must still exercise final authority in the major financial decisions of the home (minor ones he may well leave to a thrifty wife). He controls the whole, keeps track of the financial picture, and makes all of the final decisions where there are unresolvable differences of opinion. But he would be foolish not to use the gifts that God has given in his helper, and use them to the fullest. So you see, headship does not squash the woman's personality; indeed it is the very reason for developing and using it for the glory of God and the blessing of the home.

"But," you protest, "that is in the New Testament. What about the Old?" Well, what about the Old? Consider the ideal woman as she appears there (Prov. 31:10 ff.). Every woman should read these verses frequently, and their husbands would do well to read them occasionally too. What is this woman like? To begin with, she is called "a virtuous woman" (v. 10); but literally the original reads, "a woman of many parts." The writer is going to take her apart and look at each part of this remarkable woman. She is many faceted. She has many sides to her personality. She has many gifts that have been developed and are functioning well. Here is the picture of a truly liberated woman. She is in no way suppressed. She leads a full, meaningful, and productive life. Her husband knows how to bring her abilities to the fore. He is a good manager who has left many decisions to her. All of her gifts are being used fully *for her home.* All of this—and more—is in that phrase "a woman of many parts." "Her worth is far above jewels and the heart of her husband safely trusts in her. He will have no lack of gain." He can entrust much to her without fear and she will produce. That is the basic idea.

Now, let us see specifically how this woman lives. "She does him good and not evil all the days of her life." Notice, she is oriented toward her husband. She recognizes that her task is to help him. She is concerned about him; she loves him and she does him good all the days of her life. She is willing to live for him. That much is clear at the outset. She is willing to labor physically in the home as a housewife (or homemaker), or if you prefer the latest term, as a domestic engineer.

"She looks for wool and flax," and "works with her hands in delight" (v. 13). There is a difference between doing the daily chores (which is what is outlined here in terms of the duties of that day) cheerfully, and the way that so many women do them. Why is it that many women don't enjoy being a housewife (or D.E. if you prefer)? Because they have never learned to enjoy doing their daily chores. Instead, they sit around grumbling about their lot as women. They complain, "Those same old plates again! Three times a day I wash these things, only to have them dirtied again! Day after day the same old plates; wash them, dirty them, wash them, dirty them, wash them, dirty them. Same old clothes, same old washing and ironing. . . ." Then—"Same old husband, same old children!" That is what comes next.

Yet doing chores is part of what being alive in God's world is all about. But such women wallow in self-pity. They think, "My husband gets out and meets interesting people at work." Sure, he does! If some wives only knew! Don't you know that your husband has his chores too? "Who are you to talk?" you ask. "You meet interesting people all the time as a counselor." Sure! Hour after hour I listen to women pouring it into my ear about how bad it is with them at home! Come off it! Everybody has difficulties. In a world of sin everybody has problems. A man's life isn't any easier than yours. It isn't any more adventuresome or romantic than yours. What really counts is whether or not you can learn to delight in your work, whatever your task is. The same is true for your husband.

The Biblical picture of the liberated woman describes her as one who has learned to do her job *in delight*. She has learned to hum and sing while doing her dishes. She is thankful for the food that dirties the dishes.

Probably as a man I should not make the following suggestion, but I will. Perhaps you will dismiss it as typical male foolishness. That is your privilege, and perhaps you will be right. If from, say, age twenty to age seventy (to round off the figures) I had to count on the possibility of doing fifty years of cooking, I think that I would want to know a lot more about cooking than most women do. I am not criticizing the final product, you understand. But, for one thing, most women don't even know *why* water boils. They certainly know little or nothing of the chemical reactions that occur between various foods and seasonings. If I had to face cooking day after day the way that you do, with only recipes at my fingertips, I might not sing so loudly either. If I had to cook for the rest of my life in that way, I might find it hard to do so in delight. I think that I would try to learn at least something about the chemistry of cooking, at least the elementary chemistry involved, so that I would have some idea about why, in cooking, the chemicals react as they do. Then cooking might begin to get exciting. You could begin to experiment a little bit. You would be able to go beyond the recipe books without fear of poisoning the family.

"Sounds like a typical male approach," you say. Maybe so, but I offer the suggestion anyway. At any rate, the more you put into cooking, the more you will get out of it. You will enjoy cooking if you really throw yourself into it. Ada L. Roberts wrote a book called *Favorite Breads from Rose Lane Farm*.[1] It is fantastic; indeed it stands without an equal. This

---

[1] Ada Lou Roberts, *Favorite Breads from Rose Lane Farm* (New York: Hearthside Press, 1960).

woman was interested in the chemistry used in making breads. Her innovations have led to real improvements in bread making. Here was a woman who began to ask herself, Why do you put the usual ingredients in bread? Why not others? Why use them in one order and not in another? She got hold of her son's grade school science textbook and discovered, for example, that salt retards the growth of yeast. Moving out on this and other basic ideas, she invented new procedures and pioneered in the use of new ingredients. It is a great book; I know because I have eaten the bread! Mrs. Roberts did a little thinking, used a little originality, and had a marvelous time learning to bake breads that are far superior. Now why didn't you do that? Make your regular chores a pleasure; throw yourself into them with enthusiasm. You must work with your hands in delight.

Next, the ideal woman is compared to merchant ships. She is like merchant ships because she brings her food from afar. Great-grandmother had to do the same. She had to go out every day to get her food because there was no refrigeration. There are places in the world today where every day a large part of a woman's time is spent getting food for her family. She must hunt far and wide for the best bargains and the finest quality. That is how she is like the merchant ship. Because all of this takes time, she has to rise while it is still dark to "give food to her household and portions to her maidens." "Aha!" you say, "she had maidens!" I know what you're thinking: "If I had maidens I could accomplish as much as she did too." Come now, you have maidens like she never dreamed about: refrigerators, freezers, automatic washers, dryers, dishwashers. . . . Why there is a switch for everything in the kitchen except the children! And your "maidens" don't talk back either. So that won't let you off the hook; not for a moment.

She "considers a field and buys it." This woman dabbles in real estate. *She* considers a field and *she* buys it. She has great ability and her husband recognizes this. As a good manager, evidently he has agreed that she may handle such matters on her own. Now this woman certainly doesn't look squashed.

Her business ability is used for the benefit of her home. Notice: "With her earnings she plants a vineyard." She is not only buying real estate, she is going to make it productive out of money that *she* has earned previously. She "girds herself with strength and makes her arms strong." She will have to do so if she is going to work in this vineyard. "She senses that her gain is good. Her lamp does not go out at night." She makes it pay; but to do so she must work late into the evening.

"She stretches out her hands to the distaff, her hands grasp the spindle." Because of this, "she extends her hands to the poor. She stretches out her hands to the needy." That is a beautiful couplet (vv. 19, 20): stretching out her hands to her work makes it possible to stretch out her hands to those who are in need.

She is "not afraid of the snow for her household"; they are "clothed with scarlet." She has made red flannels for them! She also *makes* fine clothing for herself. Her garments are of "fine linen and purple." This woman goes down to the store, gets her Simplicity patterns, sits down to her slant-needle Singer, and goes to work on some mill ends. She is in style and able to wear fine clothing because she produced it herself.

Now take a look at her husband: he is "known in the gates where he sits among elders of the land." Please don't misunderstand that passage. The picture is not that of a wife slaving away at home all day while her husband sits around loafing. "Gates" in Scripture refers to the city hall, the place of local government. The idea is that her husband, *because* he has a wife like her, has risen to a place of prominence in the city. That is the point. He has become a city elder. He is one of the chief men of the city; she has faithfully helped him rise to this position.

She makes linen garments and sells them; she also supplies belts to the tradesmen. She has several businesses on the side. She dabbles in real estate. She has a vineyard. She makes belts and garments for sale. The idea that women should not hold jobs is false. Here is a prominent city elder's wife who does. The key to whether a job is fitting or not lies solely in whether the job helps or hinders her family.

"Strength and dignity are her clothing. And she smiles at the future. She opens her mouth in wisdom. The teaching of kindness is on her tongue." This woman is not a drudge around the house. Nor is she merely a sharp business woman. She is also intellectually alive. And she is not just intellectually green; she knows how to apply her thoughts to people's lives *with wisdom*. In Proverbs, wisdom is clearly divine wisdom. What she knows, she uses wisely so that she becomes a blessing and benefit to others. Others come to hear what she has to say.

"She looks well into the ways of her household. She does not eat the bread of idleness." That is obvious.

> Her children rise up and bless her, her husband also praises her saying, "many daughters have done nobly, but you excel them all." Charm is deceitful and beauty is vain, but a woman who fears the Lord, she shall be praised. Give her the product of her hand and let her works praise her in the gates (vv. 28-31).

I say to you, this Old Testament ideal is that of a liberated woman. Argue the point, if you want, argue it any way you care to. That woman is happy! The fact rings out in every verse. She is truly "fulfilled," to use the modern word. She is a *woman,* in every sense of that great word. Every gift that she has received from God has been developed and is being used. Her personality is not squashed. She is not dragged around by the hair by her husband. The Biblical picture is that of a liberated woman submitting joyfully to the headship of her husband and living cheerfully for him. She is deeply involved in the exciting project of discovering all that God meant for a woman to be when He made her to be her husband's helper. She is his helper not just in physical work, such as doing the dishes, but also in thinking through problems, and making decisions. Indeed, she helps in every way possible. Her husband uses her help to the full. But when it comes to a final decision and she says, "I don't think we should move," and he says "I think we should," he must make the decision and she must submit. After every factor has been fully considered and he still says yes, she knows that the decision has been made. That is submission. It does not mean failure to talk, to suggest, or even to persuade (in a submissive manner). It means that the husband bears the ultimate responsibility for the home and that she is willing to have it so.

Somebody must have the final say. Somebody must be responsible to God for the family's decisions. Where everybody is responsible, there really isn't anybody who is responsible. Any organization must have a point where the buck stops. In the home, which is an organization, it stops not with the wife, but with the husband. It is his job to oversee all, make sure that everything runs the way God says it should, and his wife must help him to do so.

As manager, your husband bears many fearful responsibilities. Perhaps the most perplexing and most difficult of all is his responsibility for managing you! Think about that for a while. If you think it is a difficult job to submit, think about his job. He must manage you. Is it possible? Is it possible to manage a woman? The answer is yes. That answer is found right here in Ephesians 5, but it must wait until the next chapter. The question now is simply this: regardless of whether your husband assumes his responsibility or not, Christian wife, are you submissive? Before God you are responsible to submit.

You must submit even if your husband fails in his role. Peter makes this point in his first letter (chapter 3). We must consider this in detail later on. Whether he does his part or not, God requires you to submit to your husband in everything as to the Lord. The only exception to that rule is if your husband should ever require you to do something that is a direct violation of a plain commandment of God. Then he no longer acts with the authority of God. As the disciples said when they were forbidden to preach, "We must obey God rather than man." Two conflicting authorities are mentioned: the authority of *God* and the authority of *man*. At that point the state was not using its authority from God; it was using the authority of man. God's authority never contradicts itself. Where such conflict arises, it is because there are two authorities in conflict, not one. God does not act against His own authority. Take, as an example, the marriage of two unbelievers. They have been pretty wild and in the past they have engaged in wife-swapping. Now one of them becomes a Christian. Let's say that it is the wife. One night her unbelieving husband says, "Let's do some more swinging." He is asking her to violate a clear commandment of God: "You must not commit adultery." In a submissive attitude she must refuse. She must obey God rather than man. This exception is no loophole for women to refuse subjection to their husbands. You must never use it in that way. It applies only if the issue involves a clear violation of God's law. But such occasions are exceedingly rare.

What God requires is not easy; sinners tend to shrink from it. But by God's grace you can learn the joys of the truly liberated woman. When you learn to be your husband's submissive helper, those joys will be yours. You can know the freedom of living within the structure of God's law. Why not test it?

A WIFE'S CHECKLIST

Am I truly submissive, willing to orient my life toward and live for my husband? In the spaces that follow, five sample areas are mentioned. Test yourself to see if you have shown submission in each of these by noting an example of submission that applies to each.

AREAS	EXAMPLES
Housework	
Child discipline	
Sexual relations	
Social relationships	
Husband's work	

If you were unable to complete the above assignment successfully, you may need to reconsider your role as a wife. Perhaps repentance leading to a consultation with your husband is called for. In the space below list any changes that you believe God wants you to make in your life.

7

LOVING
LEADERSHIP

In chapter 6 we saw that the issues in Ephesians 5:22ff. may be highlighted by asking two questions: Husbands, do you love your wives enough to die for them? Wives, do you love your husbands enough to live for them? Paul speaks to the ladies first, then to the men. We have followed his lead. Accordingly, let us consider now the first question and its implications for the Christian family. What is the husband's relationship to his wife?

The page has two sides. On one side is submission. The woman must submit to her husband as the church submits to Christ. In three ways Paul says that so plainly, so clearly, so explicitly that there is no way to squirm out from beneath the obligation. God places this responsibility on every Christian wife, for her own good and the good of her husband. He says that she must submit to her husband as her "head" as Christ also is the "head of the church" (v. 23). From that point he proceeds to explain the meaning of this headship and its obligations:

> Husbands, love your wives just as Christ also loved the church and gave himself up for her that he might sanctify her, having cleansed her by the washing of water with the word, that he might present to himself the church in all her glory, having no spot or wrinkle or any such stain, that she should be holy and blameless, so husbands ought also to love their wives as their own bodies. He who loves his own wife, loves himself, for no one ever hated his own flesh but nourishes and cherishes it, just as Christ also does the church. Because we are members of his body, for this cause a man should leave his father and his mother and cleave to his wife and the two shall become one flesh. This mystery is great, but I am speaking with reference to Christ and the Church; nevertheless, let each individual among you also love his own wife even as himself and let the wife see to it that she respect her husband. —Eph. 5:25-33

If it seems difficult for wives to obey God's commandment, let them consider that, by comparison to these words of Paul to husbands, submission is relatively simple. It is one thing to learn to submit to another. That is hard; it runs against the grain. We don't like to submit; the old man (or woman) within rebels. Yet by comparison to what Jesus Christ has required of their husbands, Christian wives have an easy lot. On the other side of the page is headship. He has told you, husbands, that you must exemplify His headship over the church. Think of that! It is one thing for the wife to exemplify the church in its relationship to Christ. That relationship ought to be perfect, but we all know that it is far from perfect. But the headship of Jesus Christ, in contrast to the faulty obedience of His church to Him, *is* perfect. It is always proper and right. It is always wise. It always embodies all that God has commanded. And you must exemplify *this*. That is the task that God has laid on your shoulders.

It is plainly too much. The task is too great for sinful, weak human beings. You know that you cannot fulfil this commandment. It is only as the Spirit of God works in your life that you can begin to approximate the Lord's loving leadership over His church. Yet you must aspire to nothing less in your relationship to your wife. You must emulate Him in all your ways. To be like Jesus Christ in relationship to your wife is an enormous order to fill. You are to be the head of your home, including your wife, just as Christ is the head of the church. When you fail, you not only fail your wife, you also fail to represent your Lord's love for His church. That is why your task is such a solemn one. When you fail to reflect Him in your marriage, you damage His name. You are called to show forth Jesus Christ by the leadership that you exercise in your home.

Now on both husband and wife God laid His commandments; there is no less stringency in one instance than in the other. The wife's role exists no less by the commandment of God than her husband's. Christian wives must not forget their obligations or be careless about them, saying that only their husbands have been given the task of exhibiting Jesus Christ in the marriage. All must exhibit Christ in some sense, and certainly both must obey Christ by obedience to all His commandments. The distinction is one of roles only. Yet because of this role distinction, when a husband fails he mars the image of our Lord in a peculiar way in which his wife cannot. Christ's authority in the home, for instance, is *centered* in the husband. It is not centered in the wife or in the children. God deposited His authority for the family primarily with the husband. It is his responsibility to see that it is exercised, and exercised properly in ways that honor Christ. The wife does not bear quite the same responsibility. And so there is a vital sense in which the husband does particularly exemplify Jesus Christ through the way in which he bears authority in the home, or fails to do so. He, therefore, more grievously misrepresents Christ to others when he fails.

Let us look at the responsibility that has been laid on the husband. As a Christian, he is responsible to God to head up his family. He is the head of his home. Headship means leadership. It does not mean merely privilege and right. It does not mean merely authority to exercise. It does not mean merely wearing the uniform and having the right to give the final word. It means all of those things, but it means also assuming the responsibilities that go with such authority. Husbands must live up to the responsibility of leadership that corresponds to the position of headship. They must truly *lead* the home.

A leader is a leader in substance, not just in name. He has more than outward power; he possesses also inward power. So the husband is responsible for everything that happens in his home. Nothing must go on in the home of which he is not aware. Nothing should happen to his children over which he does not have surveillance and, indeed, the final say. His wife should teach nothing or do nothing or say nothing in that home of which he disapproves. That is the authority of headship to which he has been called. Of course, it is difficult to exercise such headship. That is where we left off in the last chapter. The head of the home must control his home, including his wife. That is the hardest task of all! How does one control a woman? That remains to be answered.

But first notice, as the head of the home he must keep his whole household in subjection. In I Timothy 2:11-13, mentioned briefly before, Paul lists the characteristics of men who lead the kind of lives that qualify them for eldership. Elders are to be examples to the whole flock. Listen to what he says about such a man. He must be, among other things, "one who manages his own household well." He presides over it (manages it), "keeping his children under control with all dignity." Paul continues, "For if a man does not know how to manage his own household, how will he take care of the church of God?" Three times in Scripture the husband is called a manager of his household. One of the passages is before us. In verse 12, deacons are also required to be good managers of their children and of their households. It is unnecessary to discuss the many kinds of persons who might constitute a household. A household might involve servants and tutors, and so forth. The point is that the husband is to preside over all. And the children especially are mentioned. His household, then, must be under his control. He is the head of all who live in his house. Paul specifically points out in Ephesians 5 that he is the head not only of his children, but also of his wife (v. 23). His job is to assume that leadership.

In the last chapter we saw that headship does not mean crushing a wife's talents and gifts. It does not mean making all of the decisions without reference to her or the children, or giving to her no power to make decisions or to do anything on her own. Precisely the opposite is true of the Biblical picture. A good manager knows how to put other people to work. A good manager knows how to keep his children and his wife busy too. Certainly that man sitting among the elders of the gate was a good manager. He had recognized in his wife all sorts of abilities, all sorts of gifts from God that he had encouraged her to develop and use. And she was using these for the benefit of her husband and the whole household. That is what a good manager does. He will be careful not to neglect or destroy his wife's abilities. Rather, he will use them to the fullest. The good manager will recognize that God has provided his wife as a helper for him. He remembers the Scripture that reads, "Whoever finds a wife finds a good thing." He does not consider her someone to be dragged along. Rather, he thinks of her as a useful, helpful, and wonderful blessing from God. She is a helper, and as a helper he will *let* her help. He will encourage her to help.

A manager has an eye focused on all that is happening in his house, but he does not do everything himself. Instead, he looks at the whole picture and keeps everything under control. He knows everything that is going on, how it is operating, and only when it is necessary to do so steps in to change and to modify or in some way to help. Now, of course, that does not mean that he will not assume any responsibilities of his own. Certainly he will. Today in particular the husband's task of managing is very important. If management ever was important to the home, it is of vital importance now; it has grown in importance in our time.

In years past, the husband lived in the village community. He also worked there or nearby. He usually came home for lunch. Travel was not so common as it is now. But today husbands toot across the bridge to the big city to work and then back late that evening and go to sleep. They do that five days a week, sometimes seeing little of the whole family other than on weekends. Even on the farms the picture has changed. Dad comes in for lunch; but the kids are off somewhere to the consolidated school, and they don't come home for lunch anymore. People everywhere go off in automobiles and don't see each other the way they once did. So the husband, out of the home and out of touch as much as he is, must work all the harder to keep in touch with what is going on *through* his wife. He must confer with his wife regularly. He must talk with her about what is happening with the family. He must be sure that everything that should be happening is, and take steps to rectify what is not. God has not, in spite of the conditions in society today, relieved husbands of their responsibilities. Those responsibilities may be harder to exercise, but nevertheless today's fathers are just as responsible and just as necessary as their own fathers were. All the more they must think about and faithfully exercise their managerial role in the home.

Leadership of the family means seeing that all the members of the family are cared for. Physical welfare, food, clothing, shelter—all of what we ordinarily call the necessities—must be provided. Yet such provision does not constitute the principal area of failure among husbands. The place where husbands fail most, the place where their leadership tends to break down most seriously, is where you might suppose that it would be at its strongest. In the light of this passage, the area where you would think that husbands would be most zealous to see that leadership was exercised is in family worship, in family study of Scripture, in family prayer, in family attendance at the services of the church, in the family witness to a community, and in the family's direct relationship with God in doing the work that He has called them to do as individuals and as a family. You would expect to see great zeal for the training of the children in the knowledge and ways of God. Yet here is where husbands fail most miserably. How often it is that the wife is the sole impetus in the family for these things. She is the one who continually stimulates these activities. She finds it necessary to say continually to her husband, "Let's go to church tonight."

In the church of Jesus Christ, leadership in these things often belongs to the wife rather than to the husband. That is at once a usurpation and an abdication of responsibility. This role reversal brings dire consequences. Consider what it does to children. How do children learn? What do children learn? They learn largely by example. They learn that the church is for women. They learn that men can do without it. They learn that Christianity is not a very manly religion; it is fine for little children and women, but men can take it or leave it. As though Christianity were unmanly! That is part of the modern problem. Men today have the idea that Christianity is not altogether manly. There are many men who grow up with that kind of picture of Christianity. The artists' pictures of Christ often represent Him as an emaciated individual, weak, and effeminate. Surely the Christ of the artists never could have endured those last days before His death, particularly that last night. He was no weakling! But those pictures observed year by year and generation by generation have eroded the concept of a manly Christ.

The liberal do-gooders have added to the problem. Their weak Caspar Milquetoast antics did not originate with the virile Savior who came to die on the cross for His people, who fought the devil, won the victory, and broke the bands of death. Their views grossly misrepresent the manly side of Christianity. That kind of an effeminate Christianity goes along with what we hear in *Jesus Christ Superstar* today. Jesus Christ is questioned continually throughout the record: "Who are you, who are you?" There is no manly response. There is no resurrection, no victory; nothing in this record accurately depicts the powerful figure who fought the last enemy and defeated him. Instead, He remains among the dead, defeated, Himself questioning. Christ is looked on as something less than the real man and the very God that He is. Scripture presents Him as a man as well as God—but not only a man. As man He grew up in a carpenter shop before the advent of power tools. He must have developed strong biceps and muscles. One day He walked into that area in the temple where the money changers were polluting the worship of God and drove them out. He kicked over their tables and let the pigeons fly, but the people didn't resist. There is no indication in that passage that they failed to resist because of some miraculous power. Indeed, the passage seems to indicate just the opposite. The power and authority of a *man* who was right before God is what they saw, and they quivered and fled. For Christ is a man. No one can read the twenty-third chapter of the Gospel of Matthew, where He rebukes the scribes and Pharisees and says, "Woe to you, scribes and Pharisees," woe, woe, woe again and again, without seeing a man who was confronting sin head on with all the manliness of one who had the power of a sinless life. That manhood is seen in tenderness, too. Christ is a man who was not afraid to weep over the death of a friend whom He dearly loved. Christ is a *man.* Fathers who seek to emulate His headship must be men.

Christianity is a manly religion. It has a Savior who was so much of a man that He died. He did not fear death. In spite of all of the horrors of the cross, the physical tortures involved, and the agony of being rejected by God, He set His face toward Jerusalem like flint. On He went to bear the guilt and the penalty and the wrath of God in the stead of His people. Those who put their trust in Him find life through

His death. He was a man, a man who loved so dearly that He was willing to give His life for His people, for the church that is represented by the Christian wife. In Ephesians 5, the type and antitype move back and forth so closely in the mind of Paul that later on he is forced to explain: "I am speaking at this point with reference to Christ and the church." Paul so closely merged the two in his thought that he tended also to merge them in his writing.

The husband's headship must reflect Christ's headship over the church in the love of Jesus Christ for His church. Headship, then, is not just authority. Nor is it merely leadership in which one assumes responsibility. It is also a *loving* leadership so deeply influenced by the love of Jesus Christ that the husband is at length able to love his wife as Christ loved the church; that is, enough to die for her.

Notice, when Paul says that "the husband is the head of the wife as Christ is the head of the church," it is the kind of headship that Jesus Christ exercises over the church that he is talking about. Look back to Ephesians 1:22, where Paul describes that headship of Christ over the church. If a husband wants to know what headship over his wife must be like, how it parallels the headship of Christ over the church, he can find out in this verse. It says: "God put all things in subjection under his feet and gave him as head over all things to [or better, for] the church, which is his body." In other words, all things that have been given to Jesus Christ are given to Him for His church, and He exercises headship over His church for her blessing, for her benefit, and for her good. The power, authority, glory, honor, and headship at the very right hand of the Father have been given to Him that He may exercise and mediate them for His church. His headship is a headship oriented toward the church. The church is His body. The head feeds the body, nourishes the body, and cares for the body. The head doesn't run off on its own, but the head is always concerned about the body. Always sending out the messages that will bring restoration and provide for the safety and welfare of the various parts of the body, the head preserves and cares for the body.

The headship of Jesus Christ involves a deep concern for the church. That is the kind of leadership that husbands are called to exercise over their wives. They are heads over wives *as Christ is head* over His church. And that means that they do not exercise an independent headship, standing aloof on a pedestal while the wives kneel and scrape on the floor beneath. Rather, it is a headship that ministers to the wife, a headship that is concerned about her. It is a headship in love that is oriented toward doing all that one can for his wife. Christ loved the church enough to die for her. Will He not freely give her all things then? Of course, says Paul. And so it should be for one's wife. No tyrannical or arbitrary headship is allowed. Headship means love; that is, the giving of oneself.

A husband is no longer single; he may live no longer for himself. Even the single person of course must not do that. A husband has a serious obligation to his wife. It is his task (and joy) in all of his decisions to bring his wife into focus. He must make decisions in reference to his wife. As Christ acts with His church in view, the husband must act with his wife in mind. He must care for her. He must love her dearly, as Christ loves His church. Headship itself, which at first might seem to be such an offensive thing to the wife, instead turns out to be benevolent and glorious.

Paul next speaks of loving one's wife as oneself, indeed, as one's own body. The church is the body of Christ who is the head, and the wife is like the body. Paul also says to husbands, she is like *your* body. Paul makes the point from the Old Testament, quoting Genesis 2:24. His point is that once a man leaves his father and mother and cleaves to his wife, he and his wife become one flesh. This is such an intimate relationship that to love one's wife virtually is to love oneself. Whenever the husband does anything for his wife, it affects himself. His wife is so close to him, so much a part of him, that she is like his body. That is his point. And so he says, "Husbands ought also to love their wives as their own bodies. He who loves his own wife loves himself." The relationship is so close that he can hurt himself by hurting his wife. On the other hand, he only helps himself when he helps his wife.

That is true in a hundred ways. A happy wife means a happy husband. The husband who loves his wife receives love in return.

Paul continues, "No one ever hated his own flesh, but he nourishes and cherishes it, just as Christ does the church." The two most tender Greek words Paul could muster are found in this verse: nourish and cherish. Now husbands know how to nourish and cherish their own bodies, don't they? Something slips and John gashes his arm with a tool. Blood drips down and he dashes off to the medicine closet. He carefully washes it, cares for it, nourishes it, and cherishes it. He may spend the next six days nourishing and cherishing! Women supposedly can take pain better than men. Men feel pain more and seem to know how to nourish and cherish their hurts!

Yet few men know how to nourish and cherish their wives. Peter also refers to this need (I Peter 3:7): "You husbands, likewise live with your wives in an understanding way as with a weaker vessel, since she is a woman." You see, a husband must treat his wife tenderly because she "is a woman," or, as we say, *feminine*. That is what he is saying. Husbands ought not expect their wives to act like men. When husbands complain that their wives are not feminine enough (a common complaint), they ought to ask whether they have treated them as such. A husband must take into consideration what his wife's role is and what his role is. He must be tender and understanding toward her in that role, as he sees to it that she performs properly before God and her children. To be understanding, he must try to enter into her situation and see as much as he can what she is facing from the woman's viewpoint. That is difficult to do, but that is what it means to be understanding of another person: to try to get into his shoes. Naturally, they will not fit exactly. Yet husbands must try to understand what being a woman is like, says Peter.

It is hard for a husband to understand what it means when a woman gets her period and becomes a little cranky or blue. This is tough for men. They don't understand that problem because they don't have that problem. Yet they must do their best to understand and treat her tenderly during such times. And wives can help by explaining. It is hard for men to understand what it means to be home with the kids all day long every day, changing diapers morning, noon, night, and in between. Now and then it does a husband good to change a half dozen diapers, if for no other reason than to become a bit more understanding. Now and then it does him good to stay home with the kids and let his wife get out of the way in order to acquire a little more understanding. A husband needs to understand his wife's role; that is a good principle for the manager of any organization. If you manage a business or if you are an elder in the church, you must put on the shoes of the people that you are managing so that you can understand their problems. That is what Peter calls on husbands to do.

There is more involved in this that surfaces in Colossians 3:18, 19. These two verses are summary statements of what Paul says in Ephesians 5: "Wives, be subject to your husbands as is fitting in the Lord," and "Husbands, love your wives and do not be embittered against them." How easy it is for a husband to become embittered against his wife. You may say, "Why doesn't she do things my way? Why doesn't she learn to comb her hair faster and get going? Why do I always have to sit out here in the car and wait? Why does she make me late for a meeting every time? I'm ready an hour and a half ahead of time. Why can't she be on time?" Husbands can become very bitter about such things. Now it is true that you ought to help her to learn to get ready on time, but you must not become bitter about her failures. You will begin to overcome the problem of bitterness when you begin to understand her. You should not be bitter against her whenever she does something wrong simply because *you are managing the show.* Instead, you ought to ask yourself: "What have I been doing wrong and now what do I have to do about it?" You are in charge of the home (including your wife). You see, getting the family places on time is a part of your responsibility. The answer may come in understanding how much time it takes to wash and dress four children. A husband may decide to lend a hand in such a case, rather than to sit outside in the car fuming and blowing the horn!

But, let me ask, Husband, do you care for your wife even nearly as much as you care for your body? If she has a problem, do you really care? Do you take time to listen? When she is concerned about something, are you also concerned? When she is unhappy, can you still be happy? The most intimate of relationships among human beings is the husband-wife relationship. Certainly love will demand care and concern to keep that relationship close and tender.

What is love? Paul shows us here what it is. Love is giving—giving of oneself to another. It is not getting, as the world says today. It is not feeling and desire; it is not something over which one has no control. It is something that we do for another. No one loves in the abstract. Love is an attitude that issues forth in something that actually, tangibly happens. Notice in this passage, Christ loved the church and *gave Himself* for her. John 3:16 says, "God so loved the world that he *gave* his only begotten Son." In Galatians 2:20 we read, "He loved me and *gave* himself for me." "If your enemy hungers, *give* him something to eat. If your enemy thirsts, *give* him something to drink. *Do good* to those who despitefully use you." Love is not first a feeling, but rather a giving of oneself to another.

Hollywood has distorted love, the television screen distorts it, musical records distort it. Everywhere today, love is considered a happening. It just happens. "I couldn't help it," said the young man who had gotten himself and his girl into trouble in the back seat of the automobile. "I couldn't help it." He is *feeling* oriented, but not *love* oriented. He is *desire* motivated, but not *love* motivated. Love is always under control. It is commanded. Christ commands, "Love your enemies." You can't sit around whomping up a good feeling for your enemies. It doesn't come that way. But if you *give* an enemy something to eat or *give* him something to drink, soon something begins to happen to your feelings. When you invest yourself in another, you begin to feel differently toward him. Feelings must be based on something solid underneath. The feelings that develop and grow out of giving are genuine and lasting. But feelings as the base of love are fickle. When love happens, what happens when the happening stops happening? And what happens when something happens with somebody else? Feelings are not dependable; they are up one day, down the next. Feelings are not always under control, but true love is. The Bible *commands,* "Love the Lord your God with all your heart, mind, body, soul, and strength; love your neighbor as yourself; and love your enemies." And here the husband is *commanded* to love his wife.

A husband and wife come into a counseling session. She says, "I don't know why we came. The situation is hopeless." He agrees: "We don't love each other anymore." And there they sit. It is obvious that they have lost any feeling of love that they once might have had. They expect the counselor to say, "Well, I guess that's about it. If you don't love one another, there is no hope." But what we say is, "I am sorry to hear that. I guess you will have to learn how to love each other." They look astounded! "What do you mean, learn how to love each other? What are you talking about? That is ridiculous." No, it isn't ridiculous. Six or eight weeks later they are likely to go out of there hand in hand, having the feeling as well as the love if they really mean business. You see, love doesn't come, as fools believe, full blown from the head of Aphrodite. Love must grow. It has to be watered, nourished, and cared for. It must be cultivated. It has to be weeded too. Love has its problems, but real love can grow tall and strong when it is cultivated as God says.

If there is no love in your home, husband, it is *your* fault. Principally the responsibility for love in the home falls not on the wife (she should show love, of course), but on the husband. You see, husband, you are to love your wife *as Jesus Christ loves* His church. Listen to I John 4:19: "We love" (that is, *the church;* remember, the wife reflects the church); "We love [the church loves] because he [Jesus Christ] first loved us." That is how your love for Christ began. It was not because the church was so loving and lovable that Jesus just couldn't help but love her; but rather, while we were "enemies," while we were sinners, while we were rebellious and vile and loathsome creatures in His sight, Jesus first loved us—and gave His life for us! He looked on us with love in spite of it all, and determined to set His love on us. He elected us and He loved us, apart from anything in us that would commend us to Him. If love has grown cold in your family, husband, *you* must do something about it. If you are going to emulate the love of Jesus Christ for His church, it is up to you to initiate love. You cannot plead, "I can't love her because she doesn't love me." Jesus loved us when we had no love for Him. You are the head of your home. If there is little or no love in that home, it is your fault. God holds you responsible to introduce love. You must do that by *giving*. You must give your time, your interest, your money, yourself. Plan now to do something specific (concrete) for your wife each day this week. Get started *now*.

Now it is possible that your wife will fail to return your love, no matter how much you give. But, regardless, there can be love in that home. Your love for her can permeate all. If your home is cold and sterile, husband, you have the prime responsibility to change the situation. The wife, in this passage, is not told to love her husband; she is told to submit. The husband is told to love his wife. Think it over, husbands. You have a difficult job. But to honor and reflect Christ's love you must not fail. However, the fact that the husband is responsible for maintaining love in the home doesn't excuse the wife from loving. If your husband doesn't love you, nevertheless you must show love for him.

"Wait a minute," you say. "You were going to tell us how to control our wives. You have devoted all of this space to other matters, and you didn't say a word about how to control a wife." I have already told you. If you can't see that, then let me spell it out for you. Paul tells us how to control our wives when he says to "love them." *Love* them. That is how you control a woman. You must love her. She is built that way. When she is fully loved, she is fully under control. Love her. If you don't believe me, just try it.

HUSBAND'S CHECKLIST

AM I TRULY THE HEAD OF MY HOME?

Answering the following sample questions may help you to decide.

1. Do I know what is going on in my home from day to day?

2. Am I in control of what is happening; indeed, am I leading the family in the direction in which it is moving?

3. Can I control my children and my wife?

4. Do I truly love my wife (by giving of myself to her) as I should? List two ways in which I did so today:

   A.

   B.

5. Do I assume **responsible** leadership over my family?

If you did not come out well on this checklist, you need to reconsider your whole pattern of life. In the spaces below, list ten specific ways in which you can begin to show love to your wife. Then, **today,** start to change by doing one of them.

1.
2.
3.
4.
5.
6.
7.
8.
9.
10.

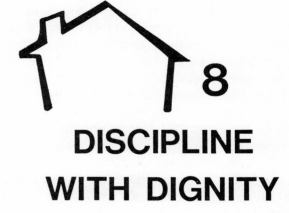

8

DISCIPLINE
WITH DIGNITY

Children, obey your parents in the Lord, for this is right.
Honor your father and your mother, which is the first
commandment with a promise: that it may be well with
you and that you may live long on the earth. And fathers,
do not provoke your children to anger but bring them up in
the discipline and instruction of the Lord. —Eph. 6:1-4

It is not possible to deal with all of these verses in detail since so much needs to be said about the problem of discipline in the home. Good family relationships between sinful parents and children do not develop naturally. They require much effort. So much may be said from each side of that relationship, that it is difficult to do more than scratch the surface. Here we will approach the whole question through the fathers, as Paul speaks to them in verse 4, and perhaps say a few things to any young people who might happen to read this book.

The first question that arises immediately as we look at verse 4 is, Why did Paul address the *fathers?* Why didn't he address the mothers? Don't mothers from the earliest time in children's lives bear more influence on them than fathers? Don't they spend more time with their children than fathers do? Aren't they the ones who all day long put up with the children's bad behavior and become the real symbols of discipline in the home on the day-by-day, hour-by-hour basis? In our society, where we no longer live in the village, where dad is away all day long and doesn't come home for lunch, mom spends more time with the children than he. So why not address moms, or at least include them?

There are at least two reasons why Paul speaks to the fathers. One of them may be that fathers have a particular problem with the issue that Paul singles out: provoking children to wrath. But that is not the major factor. When Paul speaks to the fathers he *is* speaking to the mothers. The reason that he addresses the fathers is that what the mothers do, the fathers are responsible for. In addressing the fathers, he is addressing the one in whom God has vested His authority for discipline. The father is the head of the home. The father is the one who ultimately must answer to God for what happens in his home. We already have discussed this in the two previous chapters. We noted, for example, that Paul says that a husband must "manage his own household well, keeping his children under control with all dignity" (I Tim. 3:4-5).

Now when Dad manages his household he does not always

need to administer discipline directly. He must discipline the children largely through his wife. He may have used a tutor or a servant in his household in Biblical days; today he may give some of his authority to a Christian school teacher. There are a number of ways in which he might manage his own household. Yet in all, the father must remain in control and be aware of what happens. God holds *him* responsible. So when Paul says "fathers," he is not speaking to the fathers alone. He speaks to the fathers of their responsibility to see to it that their children are properly trained.

Certainly this means that the fathers themselves should take a tremendous amount of direct responsibility for the training of their children. A number of passages give a clear indication that this is exactly what God expects. In Deuteronomy 6, for example, the fathers again are especially singled out as the ones who must answer any questions that their children may have about the faith. Obviously, this does not prohibit mothers from doing so too (cf. II Tim. 1:5; Titus 2:3-5). The fathers not only must answer questions, but, in addition, they must teach their children about God. They must impress on them the laws, ordinances, and commandments of God and explain these to their children. They must teach them not only in formal ways, but also in informal ways: when they are lying down, standing up, walking by the way; in short, in all of life's circumstances. They must teach out of the milieu. The Bible pictures the father himself frequently with his children, teaching both formally and informally. So the fathers are not exempted from personal, direct teaching because they are called managers. Yet the father cannot do all personally. The father is finally responsible for all the discipline, all the training, and all the relationships in his home. It is the father that God ultimately will hold responsible for what happened in his home. That is why Paul addresses the fathers.

Take the situation, for example, where the father is a member of one congregation but his wife and his children are members of another. In the former congregation the Bible is taught and believed; in the latter it is not The wife is supporting unbelief and the children are being instructed in liberal doctrine. This father is failing to take the lead in that home. He should take steps to bring his family together. He must insist that the instruction of his children is Scriptural.

What is it that fathers must do to discipline their children? Negatively, Paul first says, "Do not provoke your children to anger." Fathers must guard against allowing either themselves, their wives, or anyone else in the family to provoke their children to anger. In the parallel passage in Colossians 3:21, it is instructive to compare the word that is used rather than "anger." Putting the two together gives a fuller picture of what Paul is talking about. There Paul wrote: "Fathers, do not *exasperate* your children, that they may not lose heart." The term means to take the wind out of them; to take the wind out of their sails, we'd say today. Don't take the heart out of the child.

In conjunction with the notion of anger, which plugs into it snugly, exasperating children is a precise description of what happens so often in our day. As a matter of fact, angry exasperation most clearly describes the prevalent attitude of rebellion among so many modern young people. They are exasperated with their parents. They have given up on them. They frequently express a wrathful "why bother?" in counseling. They finally write off discipline as hopeless. In anger they turn their backs on their parents and close their ears, their minds, and their hearts. No two words better describe the contemporary attitude than anger mixed with exasperation. Youth have been losing heart with, giving up on, and writing off their parents' discipline in disgust.

What causes this? Why do children give up? What provokes them to anger? Notice that this verse refers to discipline. The wrong kind of discipline is behind it. After a child decides that he has had enough of it, he quits. Of course, the young person has no excuse for allowing himself to be provoked to exasperation. Yet the temptation is strong; for all discipline is difficult, and non-Biblical discipline is particularly hard to take. The fact is that exasperation often occurs when children have not been disciplined in a Biblical manner.

Underdiscipline

The most interesting fact that emerges in talking with such young people is that it is not discipline itself, nor even primarily overdiscipline, but, rather, it is underdiscipline that exasperates kids more than anything else.

Let us consider why this is true. Take an example. Unannounced rules that are made known only *after* the child has broken them, provoke exasperation. That is not discipline. Suppose the child is told, "If you do X you're going to get a spanking," but tomorrow he gets away with doing X. What happens? There is no consistent discipline. When rules change day by day, a child doesn't know where he stands. When rules are enforced only at the parents' whims, the child becomes confused. Such rules are really no rules. They tend to provoke exasperation. Such rules are not clear. The penalties are not known. The lines are not drawn. When discipline keeps changing day after day, kids finally throw their hands into the air and say, "What's the use in trying to keep rules; you never know what they are!" Wouldn't you get exasperated with the game if the rules for baseball changed every day? Yet that is the way much so-called discipline is carried on. Often that kind of discipline is found in Christian homes too.

Today little Mary comes home with a pretty flower that she picked for mommy down by the stream. She comes running in across the kitchen floor that has just been waxed, not looking at the floor but at mommy's face, which she hopes will light up in a burst of joy and gladness. But mommy doesn't see the flower. She can only see the mud which by now is all over the kitchen floor. Mary is verbally torn apart, limb by limb. What is her reaction? "I tried to be nice to mommy and I was practically murdered for it!" Mom rethinks her actions that night. "I nearly kicked her across the room; she didn't deserve that." Mom could have recouped by admitting her wrong to Mary and straightening things out. But she did not, and this led to adverse results. Tomorrow Mary may do something really serious. She may lie, give rebellious backtalk to her mother, or whatever. But because she overpunished Mary yesterday, today mom may let her get away with it. It is precisely that sort of inconsistent discipline with which our children are being raised and about which they begin to think, "What's the use?" They begin to put two and two together and find that they make ten. They think: "Today you get murdered for doing nothing, but tomorrow you get away with murder. You never know what you're going to get; you never know what the limits are; you never know what the penalties might be. What's the use? You might as well do what you want to do anyway." So, they give up on mom (or dad). They become exasperated over changing limits.

Why do parents keep moving the boundaries? Why do they keep everything in flux? Well, partly because they are lazy. They don't want to work at discipline, plan ahead, and so forth. Discipline takes effort. But of greater significance, discipline also requires change in parents. Mainly parents give up too quickly. If they say something today, and they don't see change instantly, they quit. They may stick with a rule and punishment two or three days; and if that doesn't effect a change by then, they conclude that there will be no change. They forget that when they try to establish a new pattern in their own lives (like going on a diet), it sometimes takes a long time. They expect others to be patient with them if they fail at first. But they forget this with their children. So after two or three days of trying one thing (when it will probably take two or three weeks to begin to get through), they give up and try something else (for two or three days, of course), and then wonder why nothing works. We might as well get one fact straight right now: it takes time to discipline a child. And it takes stated, consistently enforced rules. Underdiscipline is discipline that has no real limits; it is discipline in flux.

Young people want rules; they want to know where the limits are. Children who have been handled erratically frequently are brought for counseling. We talk to them along with their parents and finally suggest: "Suppose we write it all out. Suppose we write out a code of conduct. You will know the rules and the punishment for breaking each. You'll know ahead of time just what will happen. And we'll help mom and dad to stick to it. If you knew that mom and dad would really stick to the code wouldn't you like that better than what you've got now?" Invariably they reply, "You bet I would!" And when we get true discipline going, the children breathe a sigh of relief. Now they know where they stand. Now they can point to mom or dad and say, "This is what you promised to do." They can hold *them* to the code too!

Young people need to know where they stand, not only in respect to their parents, but also in relationship to other children. More than one young person has said in counseling, "Boy, I'll tell you, there's nothing greater than knowing what the limits are. When the gang wants to do something wrong and I'm tempted to go along, I can just say, 'I know what my parents will do to me if I do it; count me out!' " They're grateful for that. They're glad to be able to know where the limits are. That isn't true of every young person, of course. But everyone who thinks even a little about it will understand the advantages. Irregularity, inconsistency, no stated limits, undependability—that's the first problem. (At the end of this chapter is a Code of Conduct worksheet that you may use to set up the program in your family. Do not begin it unless you intend to follow through consistently. But, why shouldn't you?)

But there are other reasons why parents exasperate children. Sometimes the problem is underdiscipline due to too many rules. That may sound like overdiscipline, but it is not. You see, if you have dozens of rules like some parents do, you may think you are doing a really fine job of discipline; but when you keep adding rules, eventually you will either turn into policemen or (as is more likely) fail to enforce many of the rules. Either option is bad. When there are too many rules you have to be watching all the time, looking for every infraction of every rule. Every rule that is made must be policed, or it isn't worth making. In fact, it is worse to make rules that are not policed than not to make them at all.

When a parent fails to police rules, he teaches that he doesn't mean business. He teaches that he is undependable. Some rules he may enforce sometimes (usually when he's had it), but no one ever can guess which or when. That is a very shaky situation for a kid. He never knows when the hammer will fall.

Once you have made a rule, every time that rule is broken you should know it and you should follow through with the stated penalty. When you make twenty-five or thirty rules, you must spend the whole day investigating to see if the rules are being broken. You won't have time for anything else. But if you make three (or better, two) rules and faithfully police them, it won't be very long before your children get the right idea. They will know that when a rule is made it is going to be followed up.

You can teach discipline and obedience better with one rule properly enforced than with twenty-five rules that you could never follow up. Once you get results from one rule, you can introduce a second. In the long run, you will move faster this way.

You see, the trouble is that parents mean well, yet they take on more than they can possibly handle. So they don't handle it. Thereby they provoke their children to wrath. They talk a good game about discipline, but they don't really follow the rules of the game. How would you feel if every time you sat down to play checkers with your child, he changed the rules? An exasperating thought, isn't it?

The Lord gave only ten commandments for all of life. In the Garden of Eden there was just one rule. Obedience centered around it, and the penalty was clearly spelled out. Adam and Eve were told not to eat of that tree. All of the rest of the trees were theirs, but that one tree was off limits. One rule. The penalty was also spelled out: "For in the day in which you eat thereof, you shall surely die." Long before the sin, God said, "Don't; but if you do, this will be the consequence." And when it happened, He followed through.

Man died. The same was true when the Israelites went into the land of promise. God's rules, penalties, and rewards were made clear on the Mounts of Blessing and Cursing. The blessings of God were spelled out for obedience, and the curses for disobedience explicitly stated. All was laid out ahead of time. God told them that if they sinned they would be scattered among the nations. He told them about the awful siege that would take place, and He said that the city would be destroyed. He told them all of these things long before. They knew exactly what the penalties would be and why they would come. This was *before* they entered the land. Ultimately they failed, and they received the curses precisely as God had warned beforehand.

So often rules and penalties come out of the heat of the battle. That is no time to make rules. When little Mary came running across the floor with her flower and muddy feet, mother was so upset that she screamed, "You are not going outside for a week!" Whom did she punish? She won't keep that punishment. If she keeps it three days it will be a surprise. It wasn't a fair punishment to begin with. And it wasn't wise. The child could not have anticipated it because it was not articulated ahead of time. It came out of the heat of the battle—too late. Too bad!

Another reason for underdiscipline is divided authority. Husbands and wives who disagree over various rules or penalties may do so because they have never taken the time to reach agreement during the cool before the battles. Instead, they wait until it's too late, one is more upset than the other, and he (or she) wants to bring down thunderbolts on little Johnny's head. The other one sees the unfairness and in some way intervenes. Chaos and confusion! Of course it may not happen that way at all. Neither may be right. Again, there may be two different ideas of punishment that have never been thrashed out. Whatever the reason, there is only one good solution to the problem of divided authority: together, parents must think through ahead of time what they will do. If they don't, instead of really inflicting a punishment that suits the crime, they are likely to allow rule breaking to further divide them.[1]

Children are astute. They see clearly when parents are not in agreement.[2] They often begin to work on this fact and drive a few wedges of their own. They learn how to get their own way by setting one parent against the other. Yet this very result also tends to discourage children. When their parents can't agree, underdiscipline develops. While the youngsters themselves may be a part of it, they are nevertheless disgusted by it. In cases where parents cannot agree even after full discussion, the wife must submit to her husband. She may never undercut what dad has said. It is vital for her to show her respect for dad's God given authority before her children.

Failure to handle Biblically the situation where two families live in the same home often leads to division. The grandparents may want to set up their own authority and rules. They may wish to disregard their children's rules. This cannot be allowed. God has made the husband the head of that home, even of the grandparents who have come to live in it. One family solved this problem by establishing separate living quarters and separate living patterns in the same home. Another may find that this is impossible and that it will be necessary to agree on joint living quarters and patterns. In most cases, some of both must be discussed.

When children (and their children) live in their parents' home (a bad arrangement usually), there may be a jockeying back and forth of all kinds of authority. But it is the house and the home of the grandparent, and he has the right to say

---

[1] For further help, cf. Jay Adams, *Competent to Counsel* (Nutley, N.J.: Presbyterian and Reformed Publishing Co., 1971), pp. 188 ff.

[2] Often when the communication of parents with young people has broken down, it is essential for parents to mend their own fences first in order to reach their children (of course, the prime reason for straightening out one's life must be to please God). When discipline has previously been lacking because of divided authority, the most noticeable difference to children is the unity and new relationship of one parent to another exhibited in agreed-upon, fair, and consistently enforced discipline. This change alone frequently bears an effective witness to doubting, estranged children.

what he wants and what he does not want (within Biblical limits) in his own home. If his children want to raise their children (the grandchildren) in a way that is different from that which the grandparents think is proper, then they must choose from among the Biblical options. They may not fight and argue over this matter. That confuses life for everyone. They have only two options: they may try to persuade grandma and grandpa that their way would be best; or, in the event that that fails, they must leave. There isn't any third option.

Frustration methods (rather than methods "with dignity") cause problems. If mom, for example, decides that she is going to use the decibel (yelling) method of discipline, she will create frustration and chaos for all. Before long she will find out that it doesn't work. If she starts by using decibels at a certain level, she soon discovers that children can learn how to live next to a waterfall without hearing it. So she must then increase the decibels to get attention. (One child told a visiting friend, "We don't have to obey until mommy puts on her mad voice.") After awhile that level becomes "normal," and she is forced to raise the volume still more. That works for awhile until it levels off to a plateau. She continues to increase the pitch and intensity until—she gets hoarse! That is the end of the decibel method. There is no hope there; the decibel method simply doesn't work. And, it is discipline without dignity. Accompanying it usually is a rising frustration level that works mom into a frenzy. In the end the method makes her look foolish in the eyes of her children, and they get disgusted and exasperated and quit. So, then, underdiscipline is the prime temptation to become exasperated and angry.

Overdiscipline

Overdiscipline in some instances also may provoke children to anger. Some Christians have *reacted* to the permissiveness in our society, but all reaction is bad. God's Word is the Christian's standard. It always is well balanced; it never is extreme. Reaction is due to pendulum thinking that usually swings to an equally bad opposite extreme. Parents must *act,* Biblically, not *react.* Parents rightly conclude that they must do a better job of discipline. So some swing violently to the other extreme. All extremes are unbiblical.

Dad, for example, learns that he is to be the head of the home and that he bears God's authority. So he puts on his uniform and polishes up the bright brass buttons down the front and the star on the chest and the emblem on the cap. Then he parades around in it, swinging his night stick. Occasionally—just so they'll remember—he taps the kids on the head with it. Such an arbitrary use of God's authority is a misuse of it. Flaunting authority is always wrong. Talking about this authority when there is no reason to be talking about it often leads to abuse. The brandishing of authority for its own sake shows that the parent fails to recognize that the authority is given for the benefit of the child. Such assertion of authority often leads to the establishment of foolish and overly rigid rules. If "his commandments are not grievous" (I John 5:3), why should ours be?

Another area in which parents unthinkingly "turn off" children is in family devotions. These are frequently conducted as if they were for the benefit of the children *alone.* Devotions should be family oriented; not merely child oriented. Rather than giving the impression that Bible reading and prayer is for children only, now and then a brisk discussion of the application of a Biblical passage to their own lives by mom and dad in which the children virtually are ignored, would go a long way toward showing the vital part that the Word of God must play in the practical ongoing of daily life in a Christian home.

In this regard, it might be noted that children need to see disagreements between parents (they must not all occur behind closed doors). But they also need to see how they settled those disagreements *as Christians.* Otherwise, the parents have failed to teach their children how to handle the problems of marriage in God's way.

Accompanying overdiscipline is often unfairness in punishment. Overdiscipliners use sledge hammers to drive thumb tacks. Kids are tempted to be exasperated under that kind of treatment too. Foolish or inappropriate punishment grows out of this attitude. The overdiscipliner has never learned how to distinguish between things that differ. For instance, suppose a child engages in backtalk. Whenever he gives his parents lip, obviously that must be discouraged. He must be disciplined. He must be taught that this is dishonoring to parents and is a sin before God. He must be taught not only verbally, but also by discipline with teeth in it. Now, how do you do it? Well, first the parent must be sure that he avoids putting false teeth into the discipline. If he doesn't, what may happen is this: he may not only discourage backtalk, he may discourage *all* talk. He may discourage vital communication. But the last thing that a parent must do is to cut off communication. So, on the one hand he surely must discourage backtalk; but on the other he must never discourage genuine discussion, which includes giving reasons, explanations, and information that a child feels compelled to talk about. Parents may misunderstand situations. New information could make a difference. The youngster may have a really good point that he ought to have the opportunity to voice.

When he has something worthwhile to say, the child should be encouraged to do so (in the proper spirit, of course). Why do young people give up? What is the reason why communication breaks down? What leads them to turn off their parents and refuse to talk to them? So often it is because parents have refused to hear their children. When they are refused access again and again, children are tempted to respond negatively. They say, "What's the use?" They give up and in exasperation say, "I'll talk to somebody else." Parents, therefore, must learn to distinguish between the backtalk that needs to be silenced and the valid communication that needs to be encouraged.

"But," you reply, "how does one distinguish?" It is difficult to make such a distinction. But why should *you* be called on to make the decision? Let the children themselves distinguish between the two. Put the responsibility on them as soon as they are old enough to understand the distinction. Even very young children can cooperate by using a signal to flag true communication. You can say, "Why don't we agree on a key phrase or gesture by which you can signal us that you really have something to tell us?" You may use any phrase or gesture that you want; but if you lack imagination, try the navy's attention getter: "Now hear this." Whenever the child prefaces a statement in a disciplinary situation with those words, he should know that he will be heard. Not only does this provision give children a way of getting their parents' ear, but it also gives the parents a second or two to shift gears, slow down, and think about what is coming. And, best of all, it puts the responsibility on the child himself to distinguish between the two. And that is where it belongs. Of course, you must warn him that this is a privilege that must not be abused. He must not use it as a means of talking back. He may not speak in a nasty or retaliatory manner. This is a privilege designed to keep the channels of communication clear, and it ought to be used for that purpose alone.

Another area in which overdiscipline comes to the fore involves the importance of learning how to distinguish between what must be enforced as a rule and what a child must be allowed to learn on his own. When a small child reaches that point in life where he is ready to learn how to use a swing, the swing holds a tremendous attraction to him. He wants to learn, but he may seem to be such a little toddler! Yet the swing is everything to him. Mom wonders, "Shall I let this little child who can hardly walk get on a swing?" She doesn't want to do it. She knows that if she does, this little fellow is going to get some lumps, cuts, and bruises. There is going to be bloodshed; hopefully, not too much. And so she tries to hold off as long as possible, but the inevitable comes. But what does she do when the fateful day arrives? If she is wise she puts him on the swing, shows him how to swing and how not to swing, and so forth. She will stay with him until he gets the hang of it; but finally she has to leave. She can't stay there for the rest of the week. She grits her teeth and waits for the inevitable scream. When it comes—and it is bound to come—he gets his lumps. He has to learn from the lumps, too.

On the other hand, if that same child runs across the kitchen floor toward the gas range in order to grab the "beautiful little flame," what does mom do? Does she say, "Let him learn from the lumps"? Absolutely not. She quickly slaps his hand away and says no. For his own sake, she keeps him from possible serious danger. He might burn the sensitive ligaments in his hand and disfigure himself for life. She dare not allow him to grasp the flame.

Parents must learn to distinguish between *swing issues* and *flame issues.* Remember, it is easier to do so at that early age; it becomes harder later on. But ask yourself, "Is wearing blue jeans and long hair a swing issue or is it a flame issue?" You've got to ask the question. On the other hand, suppose your teen-ager wants to use drugs. Is that a flame or a swing issue? Is there a difference between drug abuse and long hair? Are there some necessary lumps to be had on the one hand and some really crucial things on the other, where a parent must put down his foot and say no?

Take another example of overdiscipline: saying no to everything. That is a crucial issue for parents to think about. Sometimes parents make everything a federal case. Usually such parents also say nothing but no. Suppose every time you turned to your husband or wife or some other person close to you, you got only "no" or "don't." Suppose there was never a word of encouragement or appreciation. Suppose he never said to you, "Say, you know, you've really been doing that job well." Suppose he seemed to see only the things that you did wrong. Suppose he never overlooked any of them in love. Suppose he was constantly on top of you about something or other. And suppose that every time you asked for something he found some fault with it and he always managed to squeeze the word *no* into every conversation. How would you begin to feel after awhile?

And yet, you know, that is exactly the way that many parents come across to their children. They say nothing about the good things they do. They fail to encourage them.

Rather, it is the noise, the shattered vase, the muddy feet, and so forth, that get all the attention. Of course, that is the easy way to go. The negative calls attention to itself, so it is easier to focus on the negative. And that is often the parent's one orientation. He is interested in weeding out those poor table manners, buttering the knife so that the peas will stay on, and all of that kind of thing. Christian parents must rethink this matter. They must not forget the times when the kids did obey and did do the right things. They must not fail to notice the times when they didn't embarrass them. It takes effort to commend the good—much more than it does to condemn the bad.

It is interesting to notice that the children's commandment: "Honor your father and mother," is positive. It is not a negative commandment like "Thou shalt not steal," "Thou shalt do no murder." Not all of the commandments are negative, but a number of them are. This one is not. The child's commandment is a positive directive: "Honor your father and mother."

The other interesting thing that Paul points out is that it is the first commandment that has a promise attached to it: "in order that you may live long on the earth." There is a promise, a reward, an encouragement. Christians, of all people, should have been the first to recognize and utilize rewards and incentives in teaching discipline to children.

The behaviorists talk about rewards; but when you really get down to it, a reward—as they look at it—is not really a reward at all. It is a means of manipulation. They have no respect for the image of God in the child. There is no place for the work of the Holy Spirit in his heart and life in conversion. There is no consideration whatever for the atoning work of our Lord Jesus Christ, who came into this world to shed His blood for His people. There are children as well as adults who believe in Him. Not only have their hearts been cleansed, but the Spirit is at work on that old sinful nature with which they were born. Also, His power helps them to pursue the commandments of God to their fulfillment and the consequent reward. The behaviorist has no real concern for the individual in any Biblical sense of the word. His is a herd mentality. Yet he talks (wrongly) about rewards more than Christians do. The commandment shows the way in which God Himself motivates children. He does so with a promise. He holds out a reward. Rewards do not exclude punishment. But it is interesting that the stress in this commandment is on reward.

Now perhaps it is vital to clear up one thing: discipline with the rod is Biblical. The use of a rod or switch is advocated throughout the Book of Proverbs. Children should be disciplined with the rod. "Foolishness is bound up in the heart of the child, but the rod drives it far from him." And as we have failed to reward, so too we have lost the Biblical emphasis on the rod. The rod is a punishment quickly and mercifully inflicted. Children sometimes at first question the word *merciful.* Yet there is no more merciful method of punishment than the rod. This Biblical emphasis gives no countenance to inflicting serious bodily injuries, breaking bones, and so forth. That was not intended by the commandment. But the rod, carefully administered with love, meaning, and purpose (as well as the right amount of force), is the most merciful form of punishment. Today prisoners spend long years in prison; and we talk about rehabilitation, yet we seem to get nowhere. One wonders sometimes whether thirty-nine stripes wouldn't do the job more effectively. Perhaps the prisoner could be released to start building a new life more quickly.

But at any rate, in discussing the matter with the child in counseling, he himself makes the same judgment. When given the privilege we find that invariably he chooses physical punishment over the prolonged tortures of forbidding privileges for days or weeks. Who says that the latter is more merciful? It is like stretching the child on the rack. And, in addition, day after day mom and dad have to retain a cool or negative attitude toward him. The child is in the doghouse. And his parents are on the outs with him for days. Is that really merciful? That is torture.

It is much better to have him bend over, "assume the

position" by grabbing the ankles (which is the safest way to do it), and get swatted. "Assuming the position" has two advantages: first of all, it gives a good clear field for teeing off with a switch or paddle; you can't miss. You get a good solid shot just where it belongs. But even more important, when the child holds on to his ankles he cannot get his hands up there between the paddle and the spot toward which it is aimed. The natural response is for him to protect himself with his hands, so parents must see to it that he does not get his fingers clubbed. If a paddle is being used, it could break bones if fingers get in between. But the swing moves faster than the hands, and if he is grasping the ankles he cannot raise his hands fast enough to deter the swat. So "assuming the position" is a safety precaution. Some parents claim that the paddle has a tenderizing effect.

Seriously, doesn't a good swift swat allow tender relationships to develop immediately after that? The punishment is over. There is no need to stay on the outs with the child for days, or even hours. He screams and hollers and kicks and cries, and then you take him into your arms. He has paid his penalty. It is over with. It is done. It is God's basic method of punishment.

Discipline and Instruction

There is also a second part to Ephesians 6:4. That is the positive part of the verse. Paul warns, do not exasperate children but "bring them up in the discipline and instruction of the Lord." God has not only told us what *not* to do, He has also told us what to do and how to do it. God commands parents to discipline their children His way. He has not left them frustrated, nor has He left them to their own ingenuity. Within the general principles that He gives here, parents must move ahead to assume their responsibility. His words "nurture and admonition of the Lord" describe His kind of training.

First of all, notice that discipline is from God. All real authority for training is from God: it is "of the Lord." But, second, all training and discipline must be *His* discipline in that it reflects the discipline that He exerts over the parent who is His child. If you are a genuine child of God you will be disciplined by Him (Heb. 12:5 ff). You too will be spanked. If you are not really a child of God, then you will not receive the chastening of the Lord. If you are a covenant breaker, someday you will receive the wrath of God for not entering into His wonderful and marvelous covenant of grace. But if you are a true child of God, you will receive the blessings of the heavenly Father's discipline in this life. So the disciplinary methods that Christian parents use should be the same as God's. They must use nurture and admonition (or discipline and instruction). That is the kind of discipline that God Himself uses. In Deuteronomy 11:1 (Berkeley), we are urged, "Be mindful of the Lord's discipline." Study it, understand it, use it.

Now, precisely what is this "discipline of the Lord," this "nurture and admonition" of which Paul speaks? The first word, "nurture" or "discipline," means training with structure. It is discipline with teeth. This training involves setting forth a program by aiming at goals and using methods that will succeed in reaching them. It contemplates patient, persistent, and consistent effort until the discipline produces a right way of life in that child. It is training backed up with the rod; it is training backed up with punishment. But it is training that also offers reward for genuine achievement. It involves a conscious desire and calculated effort to change something in the life of the child or to build something into the life of the child. That is what the first word means. Scripture is the standard for all such training.

The second word, "admonition" or "instruction," means seeing something in that child's life that you know is wrong and must be changed, verbally confronting him with God's Word about what is wrong, and by reaching down inside to touch his heart and soul, attempting to effect the change for his benefit. It means that the parent must appeal to the child to learn and exercise self-discipline. Whereas the first word speaks of discipline from without, by others, this word envisions discipline from within, growing out of personal conviction. The word literally has reference to laying an admonition on his heart, placing it on his mind. It involves more than manipulating him into this and structuring him into that behavior.

Here is where Skinner and his behavioristic methods fall by the wayside. Behaviorists "discipline" children in the same way that one disciplines a dog. Behaviorism and the Christian ethic constitute two distinct methods of training a child. Children (and wives) cannot be taught to roll over, bark twice, and go out and get the newspaper in their teeth, like the dog. Christians must be concerned about the child's relationship to God and themselves. That is what the second word is all about.

Over the years the emphasis in discipline should move from structured discipline to self-discipline. Parents must "coach" children, but learn to back off as their children learn to assume responsibilities. The Learn One/Earn One program at the end of this chapter provides one vehicle for encouraging this transition in specific ways.

Discipline with dignity, then, involves not only structure that is set up to see to it that goals are reached. That is necessary, but it also considers the personal conviction of the child to do what God says to be even more vital. He was made in the image of God, and he must be reached in his heart with God's Word. It is this message that speaks of a loving Lord who came and gave Himself for His people which first must touch our children's hearts, bringing them to repentance and faith. Parents must lead them to repentance, lead them to conviction of sin, and bring them to the Savior. And then they must continue to show them what He wants and continue to motivate them, not just with the rod, but also by the cross.

God does many things in disciplining us. Many of the key points of His perfect discipline already have been mentioned in contrast to failures due to underdiscipline and overdiscipline. But to sum up, let us put it this way: God clearly sets forth His will. He lays out the rules, and He says what the penalty will be before the infraction takes place. When the transgression happens, He follows through. That is the basis for all consistent discipline as it appears in the Word of God. In spite of our sinful failures, we must more and more train our children God's way.

CODE OF CONDUCT

CRIME	PUNISHMENT	BY WHOM	WHEN
General disobedience			

In the blocks above, list agreed-upon disciplinary rules, penalties, and procedures. When you have reached written agreement, show the code of conduct to your children and explain it to them. Ask if they have any questions or suggestions. Incorporate any changes that you both heartily agree on. You are the final authorities, and you do not have to accept any suggestions that do not strike you as improvements. When all is settled, put the code into effect. Do not work on more than three rules at one time (two might be better). Be sure to police the rules and punish each and every offense. Copies of the code, posted in rooms or other appropriate places, may help to remind everyone involved. For further information, see Adams, **Competent to Counsel**, pp. 188 ff., 220.

In conference, parents should explain the Learn one/Earn one program to their children. The Biblical principle that responsibility leads to the privilege of greater responsibility lies at the base of the program (see Matt. 25:21, 23, 29). Parents should ask their child to present a list of privileges that he would like to receive. From the list, five may be chosen and written into the blanks numbered 2, 4, 6, 8, and 10. Next to these, the parents may list in blanks 1, 3, 5, 7, and 9 five responsibilities (or achievements) that they want to see him learn. (Parents may wish to reach agreement on these in private conference.) Both lists should move from the easiest to the hardest. Laying this out ahead of time allows the child to attain privileges at his own rate. The possibility of moving up the "stairs" to the highest and most desirable privilege that is in sight often provides strong incentive. Responsibilities should be **learned** before granting a privilege. That means they should be assumed consistently for a specified length of time. Moving up to a higher level presupposes that the responsibilities assumed at a lower level will be continued. As much as it is possible, privileges should be **matched** with responsibilities, so that the former grow out of and provide ground for the latter.

LEARN ONE/EARN ONE PROGRAM

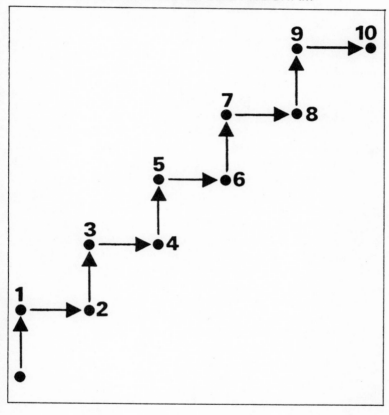

LEARN ONE (ACHIEVEMENTS)   EARN ONE (PRIVILEGES)

1 _____   2 _____

3 _____   4 _____

5 _____   6 _____

7 _____   8 _____

9 _____   10 _____

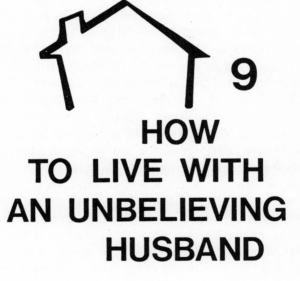

9

HOW
TO LIVE WITH
AN UNBELIEVING
HUSBAND

In the history of the church, it has never been uncommon to find Christian women married to unbelieving husbands. The phenomenon is certainly not new. In the days of Christ's earthly ministry women remained at the cross, when men fled. This is a very interesting commentary on women. The disciples had gone, but the women remained. Have you ever wondered who their husbands were and where they were? It was women who arrived first at the tomb on Sunday morning, the day of the resurrection. So it would seem that the church from the beginning has faced the situation of faithful women who are married to men who are not quite so faithful. The circumstance is of frequent enough occurrence that one would expect Scripture to speak directly to the matter. And, indeed, it does.

The first thing that must be made plain before going further is that God does not countenance the marriage of a believer to an unbeliever. In I Corinthians 7:39, Paul says that Christians must marry only "in the Lord." That phrase means *within the common faith* that Christians hold toward Jesus Christ, that faith which identifies them as a part of the body of Christ. Thus they can be said to be "in Christ," or "in the Lord" together. Nothing in Scripture in any way relaxes the clear-cut commandment that believers must not be unequally yoked with unbelievers. Christians may marry only in the Lord; that is, only within the faith.

Therefore, when Scripture gives instructions to a believing wife who is married to an unbelieving husband, it in no way countenances the marriage of a believer to an unbeliever. What is particularly in view is that situation where one of two married unbelievers becomes a Christian. This is not an infrequent occurrence. And more often than not it seems that it is the wife who becomes the believer rather than the husband.

Why that happens is difficult to explain. Interestingly enough, in the Reformed churches with which the author is most intimately acquainted, there seems to be a very high percentage of men in the congregations. For that we must be very thankful. God is blessing us richly with men. Other churches may face the problem as a greater threat than perhaps some of our churches do. Nevertheless, all of us need to know what God says about this matter. And in studying what God says, it is possible to learn some general principles about witnessing to unbelievers, too. One also may learn some vital principles about how all believers must live at home. None of the recommendations may be isolated to one situation; the principles in them cut through our whole experience as Christians. So while this chapter is particularly for those who might happen to have unbelieving husbands, its message is also for all of us. Believing husbands who have unbelieving wives may best witness to them by assuming the responsibilities of "loving leadership" that have been discussed in the chapter of that name.

It is of utmost importance to emphasize the fact that Scripture requires the believer to live with the unbelieving partner if he wishes to continue living with the believer. A Christian may not abandon his unbelieving partner. God insists that the Christian must go on living with him. This is a plain commandment from the Word of God. In I Corinthians 7, Paul speaks to the matter in verses 12-16: "To the rest I say, not the Lord. . . ." (By this he does not mean that he is speaking without authority from the Lord. What he had written previously was only an echo of what Jesus Himself had said to His disciples during His earthly ministry. Now what he says goes beyond Christ's words; he is considering a matter that Jesus did not discuss. Jesus' words referred only to the marriage relations of two believers, not to that of a believer and an unbeliever. Yet it must be remembered that Jesus is now speaking through the apostle Paul as he says this.)

> To the rest I say, not the Lord, if any brother has a wife who is an unbeliever and she consents to live with him, let him not send her away. And a woman who has an unbelieving husband and he consents to live with her, let her not send her husband away. —I Cor. 7:12-13

Words could not be clearer. If the unbeliever wants to continue the marriage, then the believing husband or wife has no right before God to break it up.

Why does Paul say this? He not only gives the directive, but he also gives the reason. He says that for the sake of the children and also for the sake of the partner, the believer must continue the marriage: "For the unbelieving husband is sanctified through his wife, and the unbelieving wife is sanctified through her husband, Otherwise your children are unclean, but now they are holy" (v. 14). It is not possible to enter into a full discussion of what "uncleanness" and "holiness" mean in this passage. This is extremely difficult to determine. It must mean this, at the very least: that other persons who live in the same home with a believer bear a certain unique relationship to God that they would not if that believer was not in their midst. How full is that relationship? How much does that believer bring to an unbeliever (whether it is his child or a husband)? This question is hard to answer. Clearly the presence of a faithful person sanctifies, or sets apart (see Gen. 18:22-33, where the presence of the righteous is said to have a preserving influence). Because of the presence of the believing partner in that home, an unbelieving partner or child stands in a special position. Certainly that means, on the very minimal level, that the gospel is in the home within easy access. The fruit of the Holy Spirit who dwells within the believer is in that home. His work may be "tasted" and His power may be seen by the others (Heb. 6:4, 5). How far the passage goes beyond this is a very difficult question to answer.

Paul goes on to say that if the unbelieving partner leaves, the situation changes (vv. 15-16). The unbeliever who was once married to an unbeliever but now is married to a Christian, must cope with something that he did not bargain for when he got married. Now his wife goes to church once a week, reads her Bible, and prays. She has new friends and is interested in fellowship with Christian people. She no longer agrees to lie on the income tax form and doesn't care to do many of the things that she used to enjoy doing. In his view she may have become an irritant. He may decide: "I didn't strike this kind of bargain when I married you. You were an unbeliever. You believed in the same things that I believe in; you lived the same kind of life that I lead. Now that you've got religion, I don't like you anymore. I'm going to find someone who will cut corners along with me. So long." If the unbeliever wants to leave, the Bible says, "Let him leave. The brother or the sister is not under bondage in such cases, but God has called us to peace." The Christian in such a situation is free from his marriage bonds and may be divorced and remarried. He (or she) is free.[1]

However, if the unbeliever wants to remain, there is the possibility of winning him to Christ. Paul says, "How do you know, O wife, whether you will save your husband? Or how do you know, O husband, whether you will save your wife?" (v. 16). One of the reasons for continuing the marriage if the unbeliever is willing to do so is in order to lead one's partner to faith in Jesus Christ. Certainly that must be an uppermost thought in the heart of any Christian. The fact that someone for whom she cared enough (at least at one time) to marry does not know Christ as she has come to know Him should arouse a strong desire to win him to the Savior. Paul says that if he leaves, then her opportunity is gone. That opportunity always exists unless the unbeliever himself says, "Forget it; I'm leaving."

If, then, there is the possibility of winning the unbelieving partner, how does a Christian do so? Specifically how does a wife who has an unbelieving husband go about seeking to win that husband? What does she do? How must she behave? What must she avoid? What will she stress? How can her behavior and words best contribute to this purpose?

There is no need to speculate about the answers to these questions. That precise problem is discussed definitively in I Peter 3:1. Here Peter says: "In the same way you wives be submissive to your own husbands. So that even if any of them are disobedient to *the* word they may be won without *a* word by the behavior of their wives." It is on the witness of their lives rather than on verbal evangelism that Peter puts the emphasis. Peter refers to the words of the wife, not to the Word of God, when he says that husbands are won without "*a* word." Notice, then, that the stress is placed on behavior rather than talk. He continues:

---

[1] See John Murray, *Divorce* (Nutley, N.J.: Presbyterian and Reformed Publishing Co., 1961), pp. 67-78.

They may be won without a word by the behavior of their wives as they observe your pure [or chaste] and respectful behavior. And let not your adornment be external only, braiding the hair, and wearing gold jewelry, and putting on dresses, but let it be the hidden person of the heart with its imperishable quality of a gentle and quiet spirit which is precious in the sight of God. For in this way, in former times, the holy women also who hoped in God used to adorn themselves, being submissive to their own husbands. Thus Sarah obeyed Abraham, calling him lord, and you have become her children if you do what is right without being frightened by any fear. —I Peter 3:2-6

And he says to husbands:

You husbands likewise live with your wives in an under-standing way as with the weaker vessel, since she is a woman. And grant her honor as a fellow heir of the grace of life so that your prayers may not be hindered (v. 7).

Then, summing up, he concludes:

Let all be harmonious, sympathetic, brotherly, kind-hearted, humble in spirit, not returning evil for evil or insult for insult, but giving a blessing instead, for you were called for the very purpose that you might inherit a blessing (v. 8).

Now, it is those first six verses in particular that lay down clear guidelines for the conduct of a believing wife in a home where there is an unbelieving husband.

Such men will not listen to the Word of God. Ordinarily the last persons that they will listen to are their wives. As sinners live together, they tend to irritate one another. All unbelieving husbands who have believing wives know that their wives are not perfect. Although their wives are Christians, they do irritate and they frequently rub their husbands the wrong way. It is very easy for a wife to major on preaching the message while forgetting about her life. But when she does so, the irritations speak far more loudly than her words. Husbands are driven from the gospel when wives continue to lecture and preach but make no attempt to improve the way that they live.

Some wives believe that their calling, once they become Christians, is to set up Bible studies in their homes as evangelical traps in which to catch their husbands. Others leave gospel literature in profusion all over the house. But as the long-suffering husband shuffles up the front porch and into the living room through tracts and pamphlets, he only too clearly gets the point. And, ordinarily, he doesn't like it; he concludes that he is being needled with the gospel.

One woman who sought counseling was upset over the fact that her unsaved husband was rejecting the gospel. She revealed her method for winning her husband to the Lord: she kept the local Christian radio station on from morning to night and turned up the volume when her husband came home. And he would go around muffling his ears. He didn't like the music, he didn't like the continual preaching, and he was getting fed up with his wife and with the gospel. Her counselor advised her to get an ear plug for her radio set and to start paying more attention to the way she was living. He urged her to show more concern for her husband as a wife and to bombard him with acts of love and concern rather than with sermons. It was not long before the husband showed up at the counseling sessions and at length became a Christian. She had been driving him away from the Lord by the radio.

It is very important for a wife not to lecture or preach to her husband (or become a suppliant who begs him to go to church). She must not deceive and trick him, maneuvering him into positions where he is constantly inundated by Biblical preaching. These kinds of maneuvers on the part of wives have been used from time immemorial to try to get husbands to come to Christ. The wonder is that they have worked as often as they have. But more often they have failed, and they have driven husbands away from the gospel. The worst thing that a wife can do is to nag her husband about the gospel. Husbands turn off wives who are like that.

One thing that a husband can't turn off, one thing that he usually doesn't want to turn off, is a wife who is a wonderful person. That is where the apostle Peter puts the stress. She must win him not by her words, but by her behavior. Her life lays the groundwork for her words. That doesn't mean that somewhere along the line she or someone else will not need to present the gospel message. Certainly it does not mean that. No one was ever saved apart from believing the gospel (Rom. 10:17). But it does mean that he will be won most readily without her continual talking, nagging, and preaching. The behavior of the wife at home is what is going to make the difference. Let me ask you: what kind of a wife are *you?* How do *you* live at home?

Virginia came for counseling. She said, "My husband will never come. He doesn't care about me or the marriage or about anything." The counselor urged: "Virginia, don't give up so easily." He began to talk about her life. Virginia saw many things that were wrong. In various ways she had been going in the wrong direction. She was failing both as a mother and as a wife. She came to see that she must change, but not as a technique to win her husband to the Lord. That can never be the prime motivation. Her change had to be based primarily on the fact that she ought to be living the right kind of life before God. She had to seek God's change *whether this won her husband or not.* The basic motive had to be changed living because God says, "Seek first the kingdom of God and his righteousness." That must always be the fundamental reason. So Virginia became convicted of the fact that she was not doing what she ought to be doing before God as a wife. She confessed this to God and asked Him to help her to become a better wife. She had given up on her husband.

The counselor asked: "What little things could you do to begin with?" She could think of nothing (it had been a long time since she had thought along those lines!). So the counselor gave her an initial suggestion: "Why don't you put candles on the table the first night when he comes home? Let him come home to some candlelight. Let him see that you really care and that you have begun to work at making this marriage go. He will notice that you are trying to be different. Just for him, put candles on the table." She protested: "He'll laugh! He'll make fun of me. He'll say, 'You've got all the lights out; I can't eat in the dark,' and that sort of thing." "Got a better idea?" "No." "Then try it anyway." Do you know what she said when she came back the next week? Her husband, Bratt, came through the door, looked at the candles, and said, "Hold everything!" He disappeared. A minute later he came back with a camera and took a picture of it! He noticed. She didn't *say* anything, but she *did* something. Conduct that first day made more impact than all of her weeks and months of nagging. That was only a minimal beginning. She had many more vital matters to deal with. But by means of this first attempt Virginia (and Bratt) got the point.

Conduct, not speech, makes the difference. She had talked to him about going to church, she had talked to him about coming to counseling, she had talked to him about all kinds of things, but it did no good. When she began to *do* something, it made the difference, all the difference in the world.

Here are some actual comments from counselees about this matter. One husband, referring to his wife, said: "I came here to see what happened to her. When she came home and said, 'I'm sorry,' I was shocked; that was the first time that she had said she was sorry in our entire marriage." Another husband put it this way: "I came here because I knew we had reached a breakthrough when she said, 'I want to submit to you.' " Because of this he began for the first time to work on making a success of his marriage. The apostle Peter says: "You wives, be submissive to your own husbands. So that even if they are disobedient to the word they may be won without a word by the behavior of their wives."

What kind of wife does your husband think you are? If you have an unsaved husband, what does he think of you? What kind of image of you does he have? Does he think of you as a nagging Christian? Does he think of you as one who talks a good Christianity but who doesn't live it? Or does he begin to see you as someone whose faith has gotten down into her life and has done things for her? As a result, is he becoming curious about whether this faith might do things for him too? Does he see that Somebody has been working in your life? Does he see a wife who is ever working at being a good wife, no matter how careless he is? Does he see kindness and love in you, even when he is resentful, bitter, nasty, and cruel? Does your faith make you treat him sweetly? Does he notice in you that imperishable quality of a gentle and quiet spirit?

It is not the nagging, but the behavior, that shows Christ in a life. The quiet winsomeness of a wife speaks eloquently of Jesus Christ.

It is interesting to notice that Peter uses two words when speaking of the wife's behavior: "pure" and "respectful." One refers to respect for her husband; it is the same word that Paul uses in Ephesians 5 when he speaks of her submission to him as God's authority in the home. But notice the other: "chaste" or "pure" behavior. There are Christian wives who have given their husbands reasons to suspect their behavior. Not just to suspect that they are resentful, but to suspect their faithfulness. In a number of situations unsaved husbands have been turned away from the church of Jesus Christ by what was careless (if not more than that), indiscreet behavior on the part of wives. And there have been wives, Christian wives, who have become all too much enamored with some fine Christian preacher or elder who is "so different" from a "wretched, unsaved husband" at home. When a wife acquires that kind of attitude, she often starts to get a roving eye. She is far from a sinless person down inside. The temptation to look at the grass across the fence may grow strong. She thinks, "How nice it would be to have a wonderful Christian husband like John," or "How lovely it would be to be the wife of a preacher like Joe." She may even begin to have fantasies about it and give her husband reasons for becoming suspicious.

All in all there is little danger of this for a woman who in every way is seeking to fulfil all her duties as a wife. She will be careful not to strike bargains with her husband with her body or withhold sexual relations out of anger. Rather, in strict accord with I Corinthians 7:1-5, she will be zealous to fulfil her role as her husband's submissive, alluring, and sexually satisfying partner. Her husband will have no need to suspect her. She will "do him good and not evil all the days of her life" (Prov. 31:12). She will encourage him to "rejoice with her"; she will endeavor to be his satisfying lover, exhilarating him with her love (see Prov. 5:15-20). How often Christian women have failed in their sexual duties and thereby not only have placed great temptation before their unsaved husbands, but have brought reproach on Jesus Christ.

In conclusion, there is but one message to the wife of an unsaved husband: win him by your life. Pray and live; that is your basic witness.

YOUR CHECKLIST

As the wife of an unsaved husband, ask yourself, "What am I doing about it?" Then list your answers below, and with prayer take whatever appropriate courses of action that may seem necessary.

---

1. WHAT AM I DOING RIGHT?

2. WHAT AM I DOING WRONG?

3. WHAT DOES GOD WANT ME
   TO DO TO CORRECT
   MY BEHAVIOR?

10
CONCLUSION

If you have recognized some of the failures in your family, why not do something about it? Here is a simple Biblical plan to help you to do so.

First, make a full list of all the things that you have been doing wrong in your marriage (take the log out of your own eye before you begin). You may use the Work Sheet at the end of this chapter. Be specific, not general. We are not careless in the abstract: we speak harsh words, throw socks on the floor, fail to hold coats or doors for others, and so forth. We live concretely, and that means that we sin concretely. Therefore, changes also must be made concretely. Repentance always has a specific, concrete side. (Cf. Luke 3:8-14).

Second, confess your sins in repentance to God.

Third, determine to change according to Biblical precepts and examples, and write out specific proposals next to each item on the list. Ask God for help in accomplishing these changes.

Fourth, go humbly to your husband or wife or your parents or children and admit your sins against them, telling them that you have sought and found God's forgiveness and now desire theirs. Be sure to speak *only* of *your* sins and failures.

Fifth, having received forgiveness, seek to rectify any wrongs immediately whenever that is possible. Where the change involves the development of a new relationship built on a new, Biblical pattern of life, discuss your proposal with your partner and request his (her) help in building these new patterns and this new relationship throughout the days ahead.

In order to pursue this matter further, see the information on setting up a conference table in Adams, *Competent to Counsel*, pp. 231-236, 250, 264 ff.

WORK SHEET

My Sinful Ways | What God Wants Me to Do About Them

SCRIPTURE INDEX

Genesis
1:28 51
2:18 .... 47ff
2:24 .... 47ff, 51, 96
18:22, 23 130

Deuteronomy
6 105
11:1 121

Psalm
4 31
127 51

Proverbs
2:17 .... 45, 50
5:15-20 137
25:28 31
29:11 31
29:22 31
31:10ff 77
31:12 137
31:30 62

Isaiah
1:5, 6 16

Malachi
2:14 .... 45, 50

Matthew
5:23, 24 36
6:34 37
7:3-5 33
18:15-17 36
25:21, 23, 29 125

Luke
3:8-14 140

John
3:16 .... 41, 99

Romans
8:28 60
10:17 134
12:20 4
15:1, 2 32

I Corinthians
7:7 .... 40, 50, 60ff 137
7:12, 13 .... 129ff
7:26 46

7:29-31 46
7:36 .... 60ff
7:39 128
13 33
14 .... 72, 75

II Corinthians
8:10 66

Galatians
2:20 .... 41, 99

Ephesians
Book of 23
1 - 3 26
1:22 95
4 .... 26ff
4:1 26
4:8 26
4:11, 12 27
4:15 26
4:17 26
4:25 .... 28, 31ff
4:29 38
4:31, 32 32
5:22ff 25, 46, 70ff
5:22-24 70-85
5:25-33 87-102
6:1-6 .... 25, 26, 103ff
6:4 .... 103ff

Philippians
2:13 66

Colossians
2:3 13
2:21 106
3:8-12 27
3:18—4:1 26
3:18, 19 98

II Thessalonians
3:10 61

I Timothy
2 .... 72, 75, 91ff
3:4, 5 .... 76, 104

II Timothy
1:5 105

Titus
2:3-5 105

Hebrews
6:4, 5 130
12:5ff 120
13:4 46

I Peter
3:1ff 72, 131ff
3:3-5 62
3:7 .... 97ff

I John
1:8-10 11
4:19 100
5:3 114

Revelation
19:7-9 46
19:7, 8 62
21:2 .... 46, 62